THE GREAT ACOUSTIC ROCK GUITAR

AUTHENTIC GUITAR TAB EDITION

45 OF THE BEST GUITAR SONGS FROM YOUR FAVORITE ARTISTS

Alfred Publishing Co., Inc.
16320 Roscoe Blvd., Suite 100
P.O. Box 10003
Van Nuys, CA 91410-0003
alfred.com

Copyright © MMVII by Alfred Publishing Co., Inc.
All rights reserved. Printed in USA.
ISBN-10: 0-7390-4614-4
ISBN-13: 978-0-7390-4614-2

Cover Photos
Guitar: Martin Vintage HD 28V (courtesy Martin Guitar Company)
Cover Background
© istockphoto.com / andhedesigns

CONTENTS

Annie's Song	John Denver	6
As Tears Go By	Rolling Stones	8
Baby, Now That I've Found You	Alison Krauss	16
Black Water	The Doobie Brothers	11
Blowin' in the Wind	Peter, Paul & Mary	22
Both Sides Now	Joni Mitchell	24
Can't Find My Way Home	Blind Faith	29
Carefree Highway	Gordon Lightfoot	42
Cat's in the Cradle	Harry Chapin	54
Cheeseburger in Paradise	Jimmy Buffett	60
Chelsea Morning	Joni Mitchell	64
Crazy Love	Van Morrison	68
Danny's Song	Loggins & Messina	45
Good Riddance (Time of Your Life)	Green Day	72
Handy Man	James Taylor	84
Hotel California	Eagles	88
I Got a Name	Jim Croce	75
Jesse	Janis Ian	104
Layla (Unplugged)	Eric Clapton	109
Lyin' Eyes	Eagles	116
Maggie May	Rod Stewart	125
Margaritaville	Jimmy Buffett	128
Mexico	James Taylor	132

Song	Artist	Page
Mood for a Day	Yes	146
More Than a Feeling	Boston	139
Mr. Bojangles	The Nitty Gritty Dirt Band	150
Operator (That's Not the Way It Feels)	Jim Croce	153
Over the Rainbow/What a Wonderful World	Iz (Israel Kamakawiwo'ole)	162
Peaceful Easy Feeling	Eagles	166
The River	Bruce Springsteen	178
Rocky Mountain High	John Denver	175
Scarborough Fair/Canticle	Simon and Garfunkel	184
Shower the People	James Taylor	187
Son of a Son of a Sailor	Jimmy Buffett	192
The Sound of Silence	Simon and Garfunkel	200
Still Crazy After All These Years	Paul Simon	205
Streets of Philadelphia	Bruce Springsteen	196
Sundown	Gordon Lightfoot	210
Sunshine on My Shoulders	John Denver	220
Taxi	Harry Chapin	222
Time in a Bottle	Jim Croce	230
Tin Man	America	217
Tupelo Honey	Van Morrison	238
Ventura Highway	America	248
Wildfire	Michael Martin Murphey	242

ARTIST INDEX

America
- Tin Man 217
- Ventura Highway 248

Blind Faith
- Can't Find My Way Home 29

Boston
- More Than a Feeling 139

Jimmy Buffett
- Cheeseburger in Paradise 60
- Margaritaville 128
- Son of a Son of a Sailor 192

Harry Chapin
- Cat's in the Cradle 54
- Taxi 222

Eric Clapton
- Layla (Unplugged) 109

Jim Croce
- I Got a Name 75
- Operator (That's Not the Way It Feels) 153
- Time in a Bottle 230

John Denver
- Annie's Song 6
- Rocky Mountain High 175
- Sunshine on My Shoulders 220

The Doobie Brothers
- Black Water 11

Eagles
- Hotel California 88
- Lyin' Eyes 116
- Peaceful Easy Feeling 166

Green Day
- Good Riddance (Time of Your Life) .. 72

Janis Ian
- Jesse 104

Iz (Israel Kamakawiwo'ole)
- Over the Rainbow/ What a Wonderful World 162

Alison Krauss
- Baby, Now That I've Found You 16

Gordon Lightfoot
Carefree Highway 42
Sundown 210

Loggins & Messina
Danny's Song 45

Joni Mitchell
Chelsea Morning 64
Both Sides Now 24

Van Morrison
Crazy Love 68
Tupelo Honey 238

Michael Martin Murphey
Wildfire 242

The Nitty Gritty Dirt Band
Mr. Bojangles 150

Peter, Paul & Mary
Blowin' in the Wind 22

Rolling Stones
As Tears Go By 8

Simon and Garfunkel
Scarborough Fair/Canticle 184
The Sound of Silence 200

Paul Simon
Still Crazy After All These Years ... 205

Bruce Springsteen
The River 178
Streets of Philadelphia 196

Rod Stewart
Maggie May 125

James Taylor
Handy Man 84
Mexico 132
Shower the People 187

Yes
Mood for a Day 146

ANNIE'S SONG

Words and Music by
JOHN DENVER

AS TEARS GO BY

Words and Music by
MICK JAGGER, KEITH RICHARDS
and ANDREW LOOG OLDHAM

As Tears Go By - 3 - 1

© 1964 (Renewed) ABKCO MUSIC, INC
All Publication Rights for the U.S. and Canada Controlled by TRO-ESSEX MUSIC, INC. and ABKCO MUSIC, INC.
All Rights Reserved   Used by Permission

Verse 2:
My riches can't buy everything,
I want to hear the children sing.
All I hear is the sound of rain falling on the ground.
I sit and watch as tears go by.
To Instrumental

Verse 3:
It is the evening of the day,
I sit and watch the children play.
Doin' things I used to do, they think are new,
I sit and watch as tears go by.
Mm mm mm . . .
To Instrumental and fade

Verse 2:
Well, if it rains, I don't care,
Don't make no difference to me;
Just take that streetcar that's
Goin' uptown.

Yeah, I'd like to hear some funky
Dixieland and dance a honky-tonk,
And I'll be buyin' everybody
Drinks around.
(*To Chorus:*)

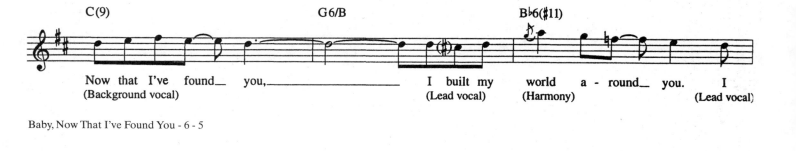

Baby, Now That I've Found You - 6 - 6

Verse 2:
How many years must a mountain exist before it is washed to the sea?
How many years can some people exist before they're allowed to be free?
How many times can a man turn his head and pretend that he just doesn't see?
The answer, my friend, is blowin' in the wind,
The answer is blowin' in the wind.

Verse 3:
How many times must a man look up before he can see the sky?
How many ears must one man have before he can hear people cry?
How many deaths will it take till he knows that too many people have died?
The answer, my friend, is blowin' in the wind,
The answer is blowin' in the wind.

BOTH SIDES NOW

Gtr. 1 Capo 2; tuning:
⑥ = E ③ = G#
⑤ = B ②= B
④ = E ① = E

Words and Music by
JONI MITCHELL

Moderately ♩ = 98

Intro:

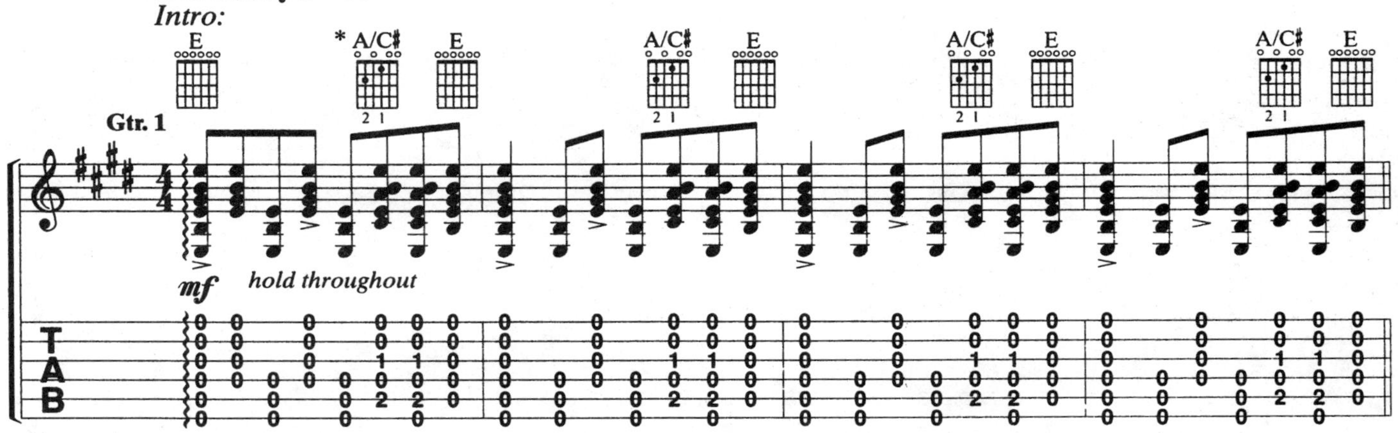

*Basic harmony.

Verses:

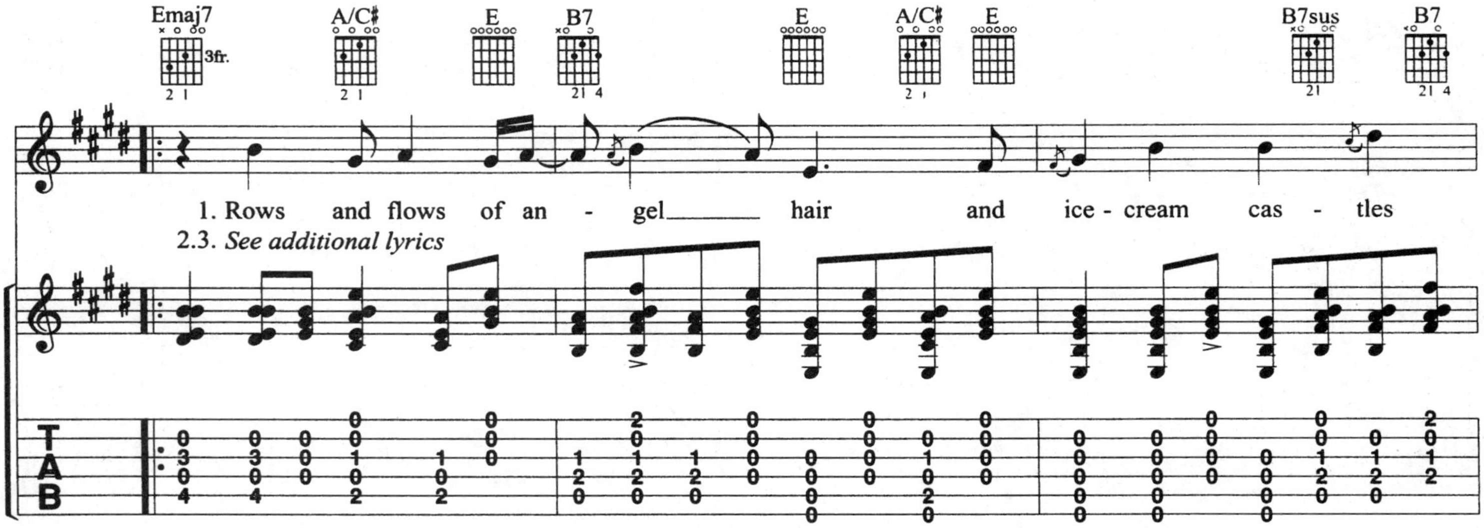

1. Rows and flows of an-gel hair and ice-cream cas-tles
2.3. *See additional lyrics*

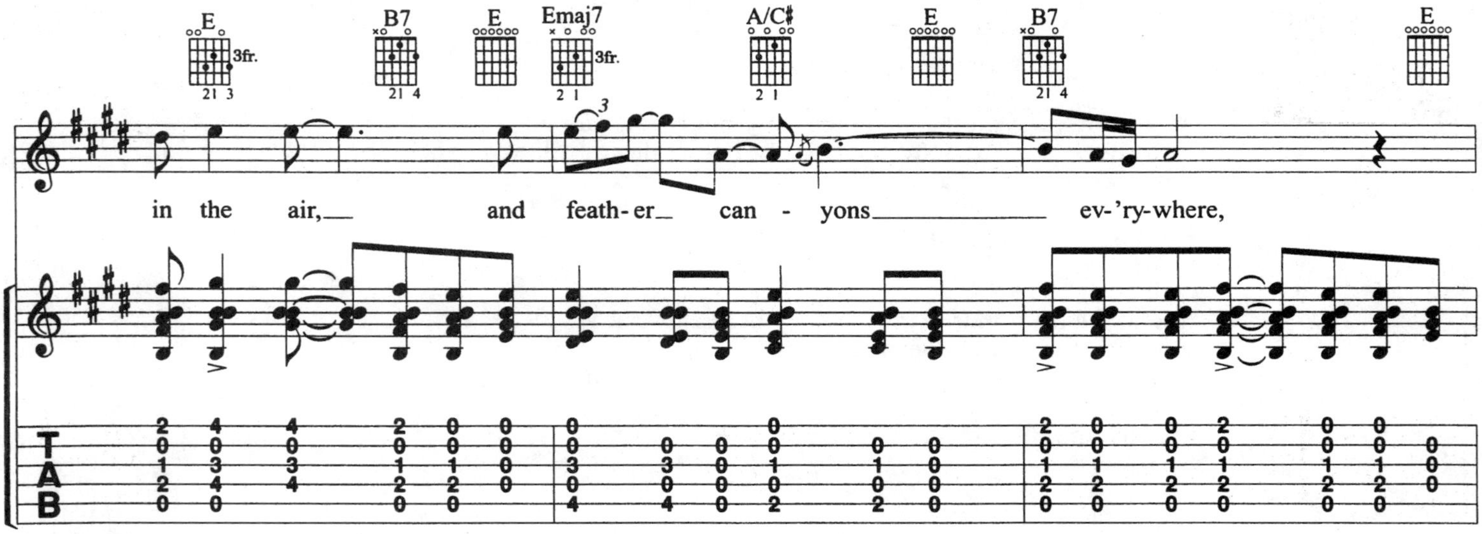

in the air, and feath-er can-yons ev-'ry-where,

Both Sides Now - 5 - 1

© 1967 (Renewed) CRAZY CROW MUSIC
All Rights Administered by Sony/ATV Music Publishing,
8 Music Square West, Nashville, TN 37203
All Rights Reserved

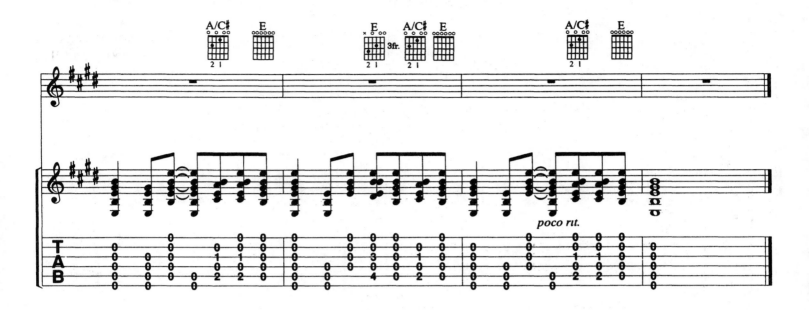

Verse 2:
Moons and Junes and Ferris wheels,
The dizzy dancing way you feel,
As every fairy tale comes real,
I've looked at love that way.
But now it's just another show,
You leave 'em laughing when you go.
And if you care, don't let them know,
Don't give yourself away.

Chorus 2:
I've looked at love from both sides now,
From give and take, and still, somehow
It's love's illusions I recall.
I really don't know love at all.

Verse 3:
Tears and fears and feeling proud,
To say "I love you" right out loud,
Dreams and schemes and circus crowds,
I've look at life that way.
But now old friends are acting strange,
They shake their heads, they say I've changed.
Well, something's lost but something's gained,
In living every day.

Chorus 3:
I've looked at life from both sides now,
From win and lose, and still, somehow
It's life's illusions I recall.
I really don't know life at all.

CAN'T FIND MY WAY HOME

All gtrs. in Drop D tuning: ⑥ = D

Words and Music by
STEVE WINWOOD

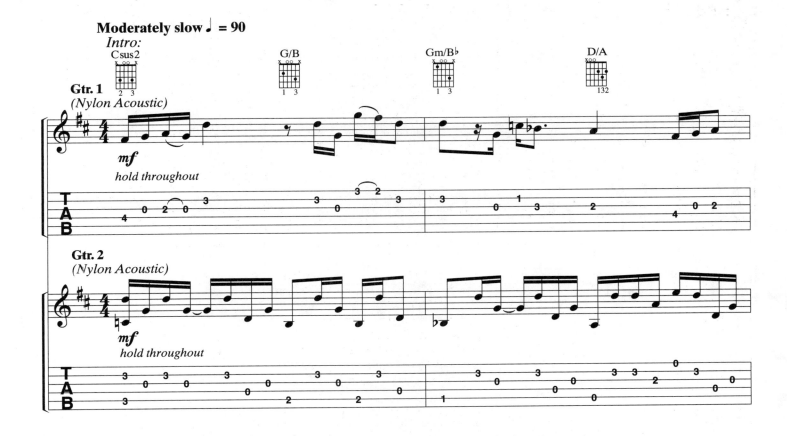

Can't Find My Way Home - 13 - 1

© 1970 (Renewed), 1997 F.S. MUSIC LTD.
All Rights Administered by WARNER-TAMERLANE PUBLISHING CORP.
All Rights Reserved

Verse 2:
Turnin' back the pages to the times I love best,
I wonder if she'll ever do the same.
Now, the thing I call livin' is just bein' satisfied
With knowin' I got no one left to blame.

Chorus 2 & 4:
Carefree highway, I got to see you, my old flame.
Carefree highway, you seen better days.
The mornin' after blues, from my head down to my shoes;
Carefree highway, let me slip away,
Slip away on you.

Verse 3:
Searchin' through the fragments of my dream shattered sleep,
I wonder if the years have closed her mind.
Well, I guess it must be wanderlust or tryin' to get free,
From the good old faithful feelin' we once knew.
(To Chorus:)

DANNY'S SONG

Words and Music by
KENNY LOGGINS

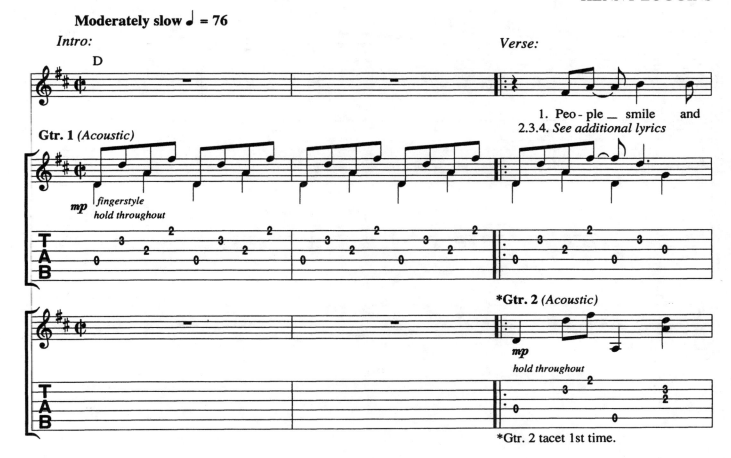

© 1970, 1973 (Copyrights Renewed) GNOSSOS MUSIC
All Rights Reserved

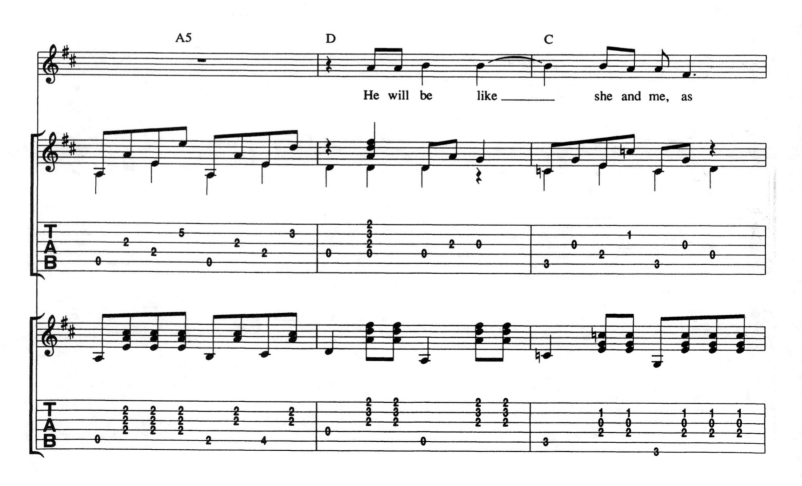

47

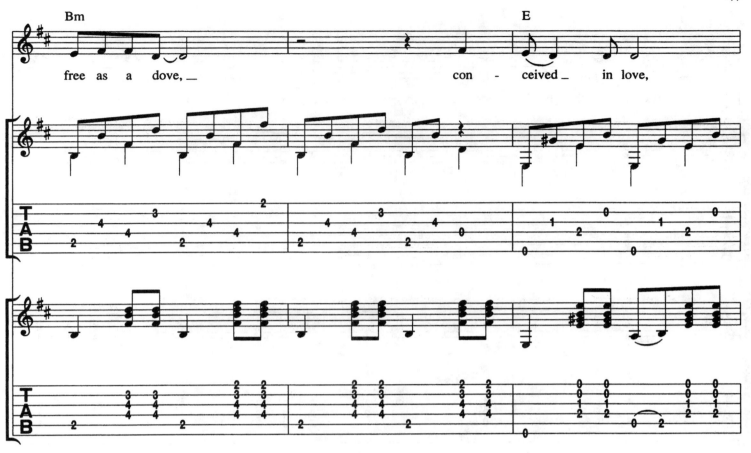

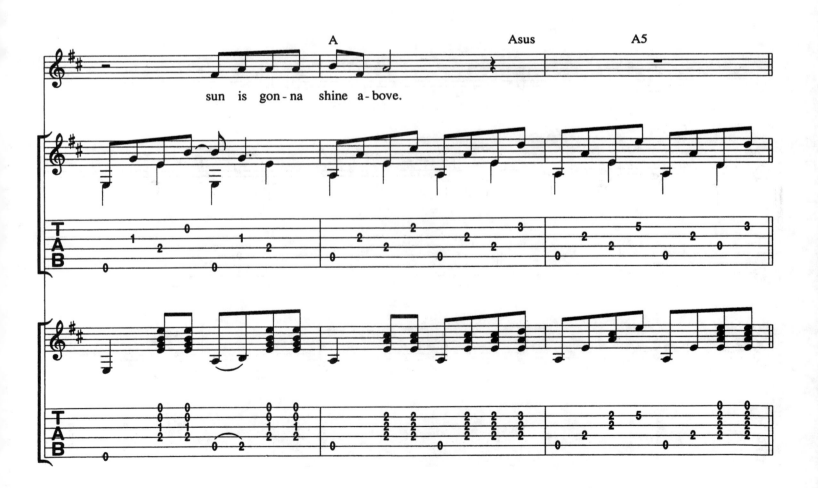

Danny's Song - 9 - 3

48

*All backing vocals on last Chorus only.

Danny's Song - 9 - 4

Outro:

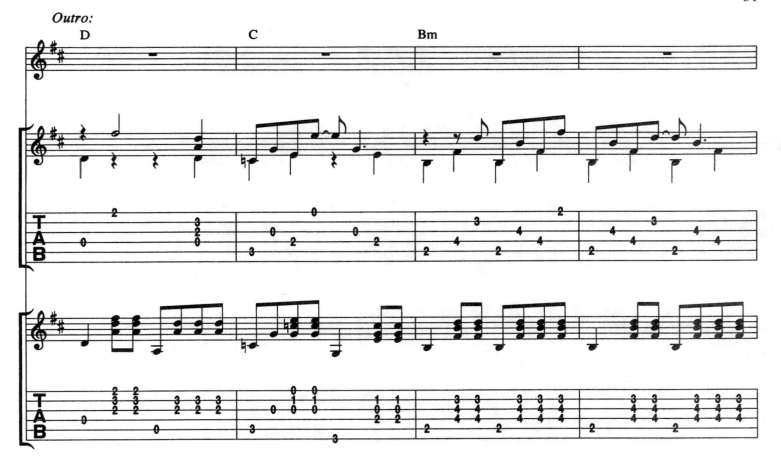

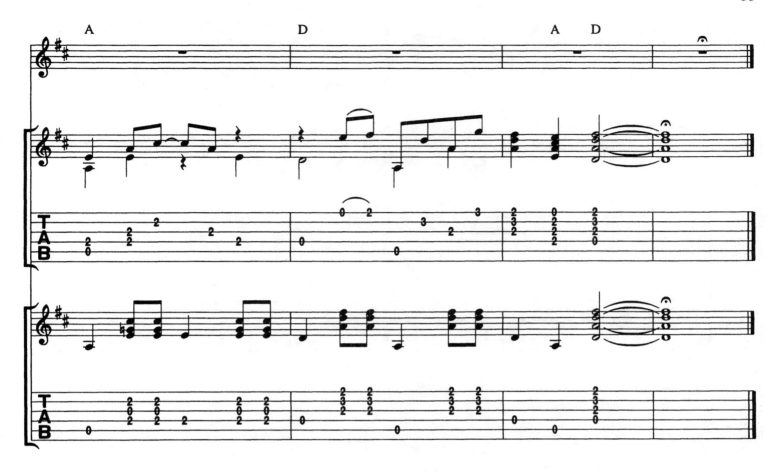

Verse 2:
Seems as though a month ago I was Beta Chi,
Never got high,
Oh, I was a sorry guy.
And now a smile, a face, a girl that shares my name, yeah.
Now I'm through with the game,
This boy will never be the same.
(To Chorus:)

Verse 3:
Pisces, Virgo rising, is a very good sign,
Strong and kind,
And the little boy is mine.
Now I see a family where there once was none.
Now we've just begun,
Yeah, we're going to fly to the sun.
(To Chorus:)

Verse 4:
Love the girl who holds the world in a paper cup.
Drink it up,
Love her and she'll bring you luck.
And if you find she helps your mind, buddy, take her home, yeah.
Don't you live alone, try to earn what lovers own.
(To Chorus:)

CAT'S IN THE CRADLE

Words and Music by
HARRY CHAPIN and SANDY CHAPIN

Moderately, with a 2 feel ♩ = 75

Intro:

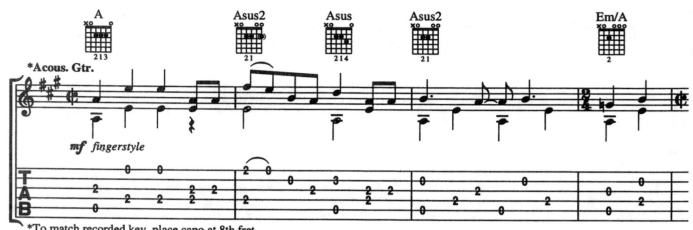

*To match recorded key, place capo at 8th fret.

Verses 1, 2, & 3:

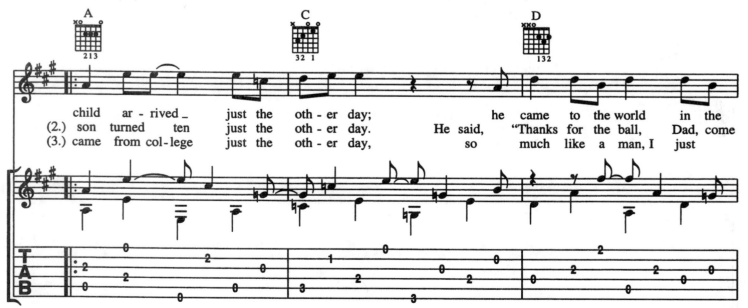

1. My child arrived just the other day; he came to the world in the
(2.) son turned ten just the other day. He said, "Thanks for the ball, Dad, come
(3.) came from college just the other day, so much like a man, I just

© 1974 (Renewed) STORY SONGS, LTD.
All Rights Administered by WB MUSIC CORP.
All Rights Reserved

58

Verse 4:

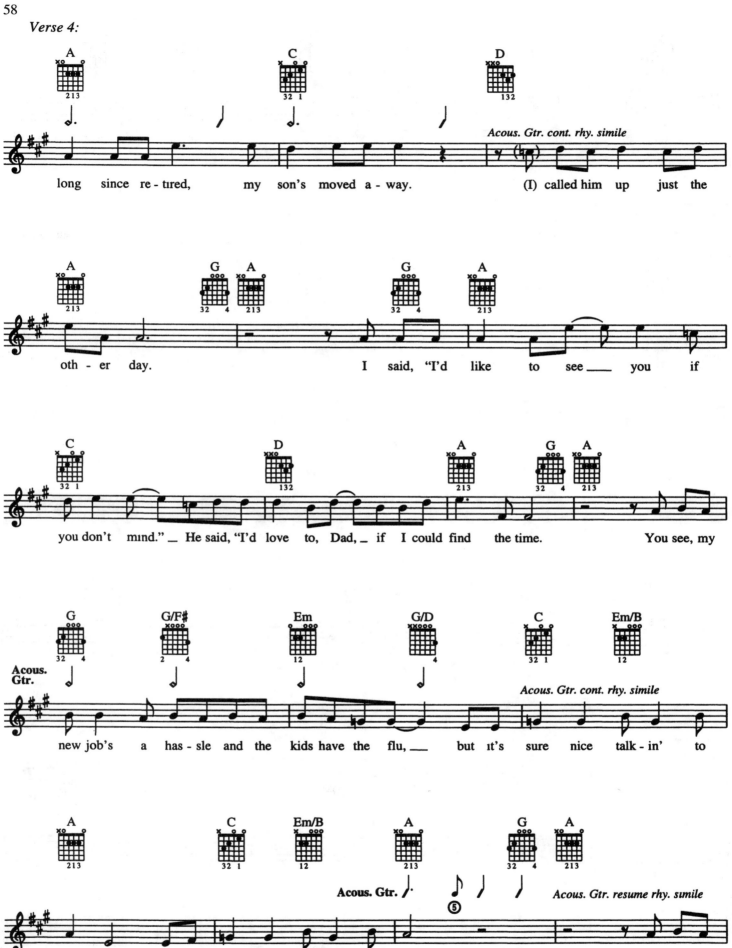

Cat's in the Cradle - 6 - 5

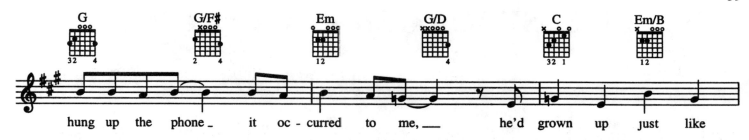
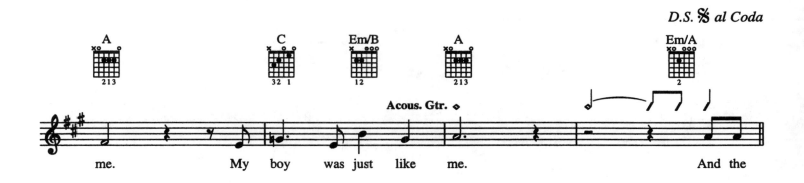
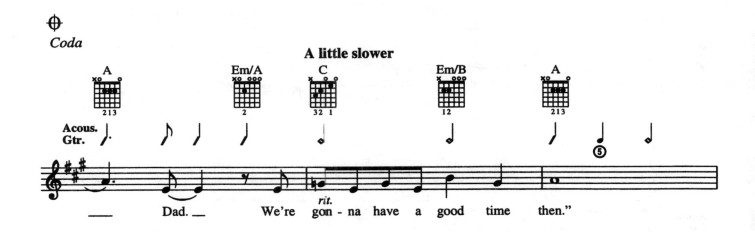
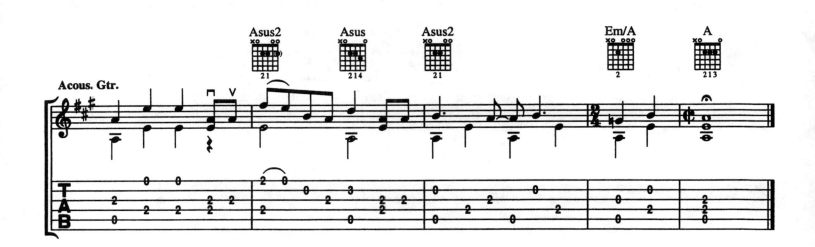

CHEESEBURGER IN PARADISE

Words and Music by
JIMMY BUFFETT

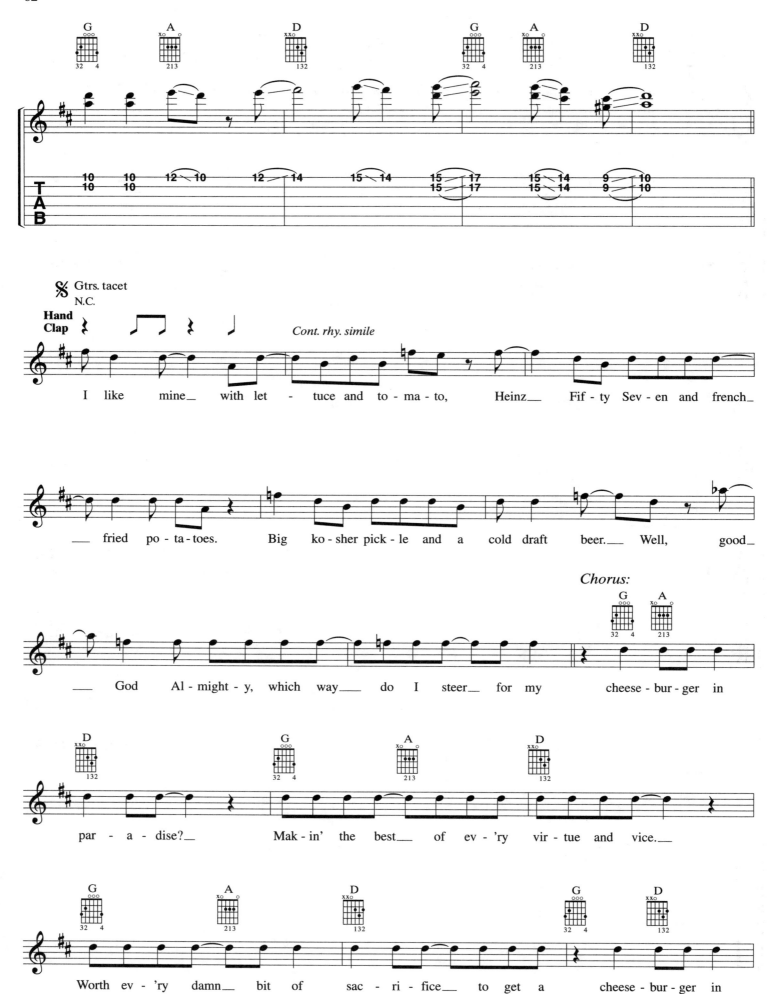

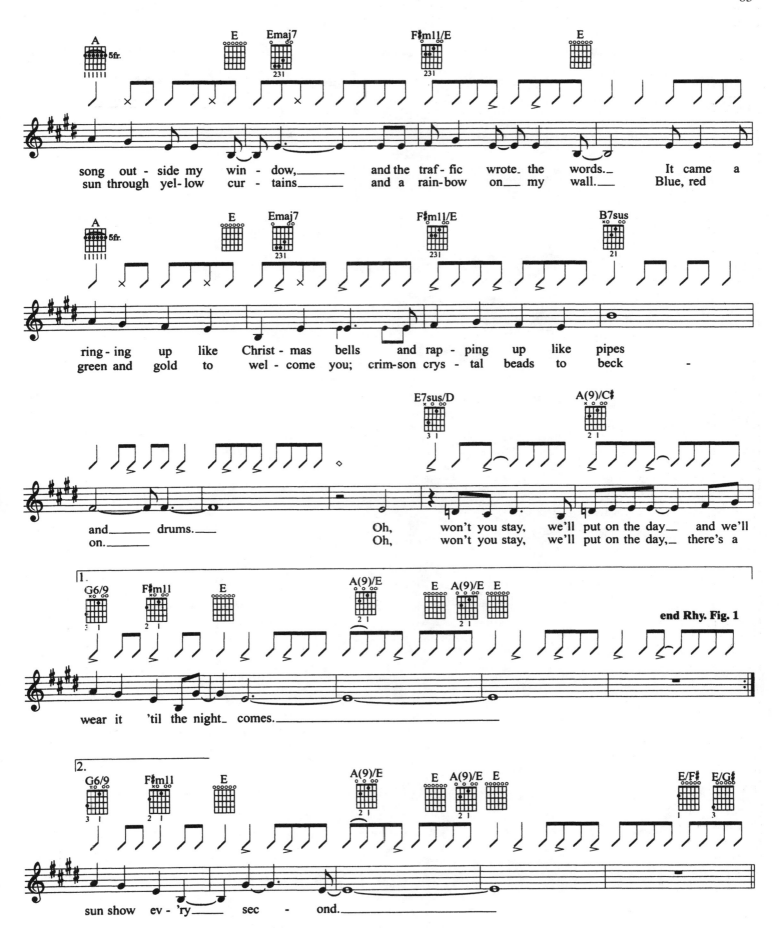

68

CRAZY LOVE

Words and Music by
VAN MORRISON

Crazy Love - 4 - 1

© 1971 (Renewed) WB MUSIC CORP. and CALEDONIA SOUL MUSIC
All Rights Administered by WB MUSIC CORP.
All Rights Reserved

Verse 2:
She's got a fine sense of humor,
When I'm feeling low - down.
And when I come to her
When the sun goes down.
Take away my trouble,
Take away my grief,
Take away my heartache
In the night, like a thief.
(To Chorus:)

Verse 3:
And when I'm returning from so far away,
She gives me some sweet lovin',
Brightens up my day.
Yeah, and it makes me righteous.
Yeah, and it makes me whole.
Yeah, and it makes me mellow
Down into my soul.
(To Chorus:)

GOOD RIDDANCE (TIME OF YOUR LIFE)

Lyrics by BILLIE JOE
Music by GREEN DAY

I GOT A NAME

Words by NORMAN GIMBEL
Music by CHARLES FOX

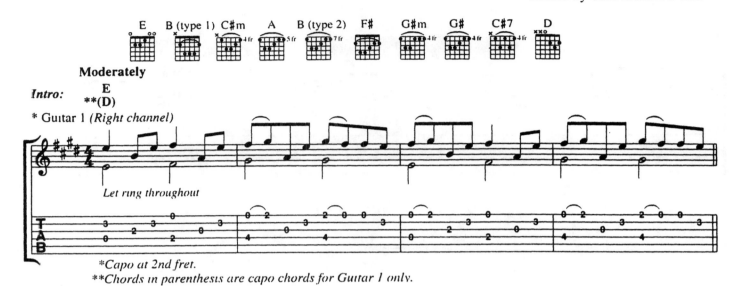

© 1973 (Renewed) WARNER-TAMERLANE PUBLISHING CORP.
All Rights Reserved

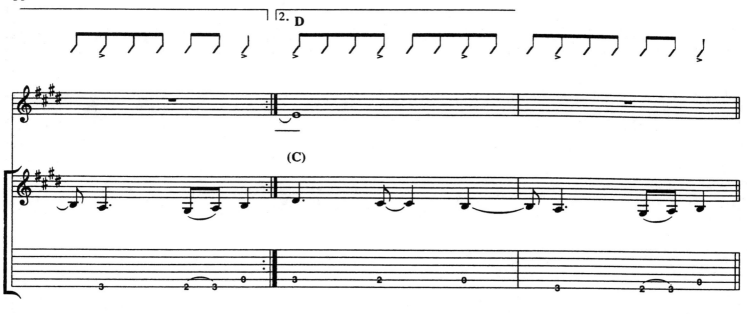

Guitar Solo: *With Rhythm Figs. 1 & 2 w/ad-lib variations*

Guitar 3

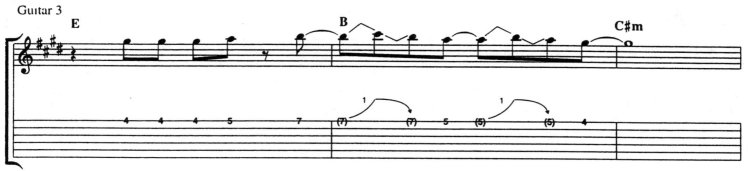

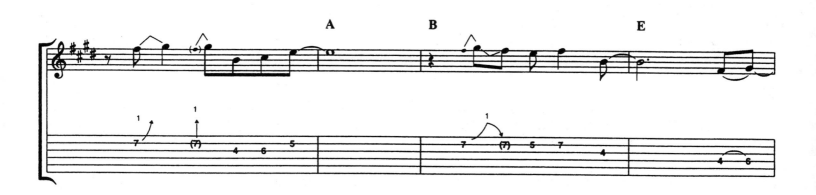

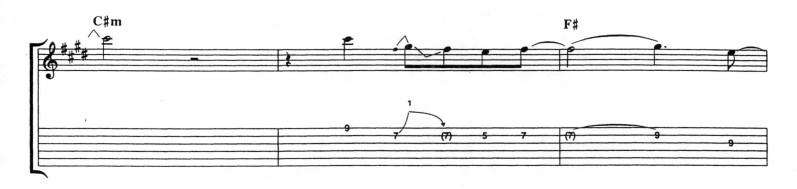
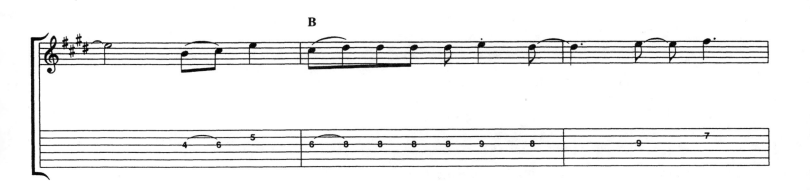

And I'm gon-na go there free.

I Got a Name - 9 - 7

Additional lyrics

3. Like the fool I am and I'll always be,
   I've got a dream; I've got a dream.
   They can change their minds, but they can't change me.
   I've got a dream; I've got a dream.
   Oh, I know I could share it if you'd want me to;
   If you're goin' my way, I'll go with you.

   Movin' me down the highway,
   Rollin' me down the highway,
   Movin' ahead so life won't pass me by

HANDY MAN

Words and Music by
OTIS BLACKWELL and JIMMY JONES

*Capo 2nd fret to match pitch of recording.

Handy Man - 4 - 1

© 1959 (Renewed 1985) EMI Unart Catalog Inc.
All Rights Controlled by EMI UNART CATALOG INC. (Publishing) and ALFRED PUBLISHING CO. (Print)
All Rights Reserved

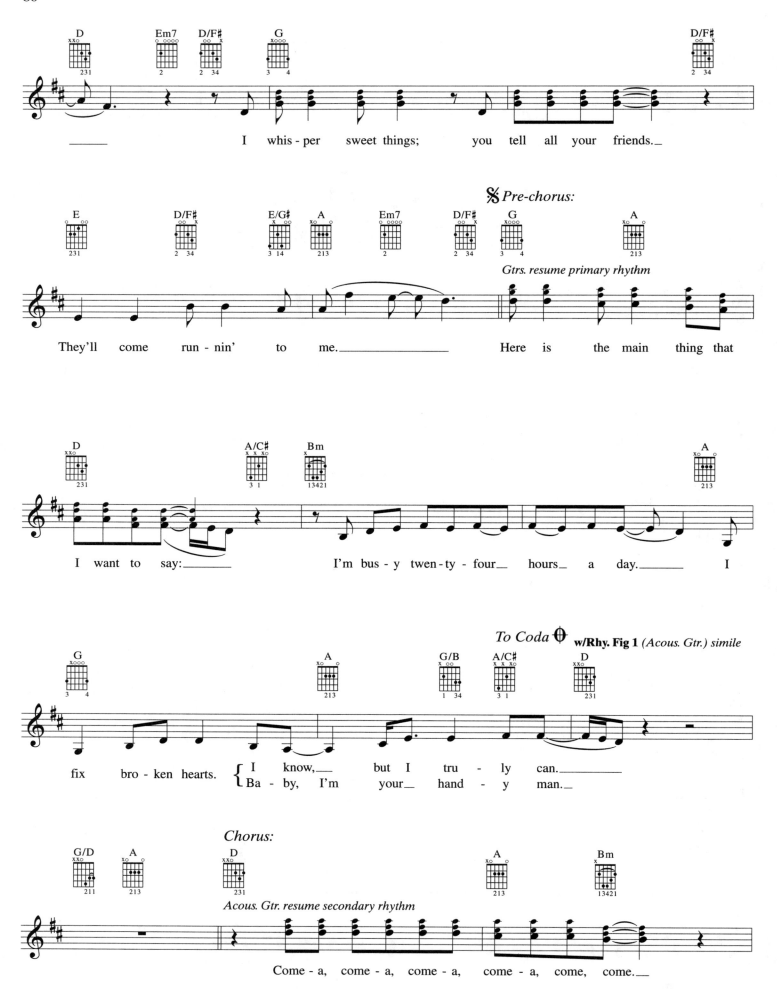

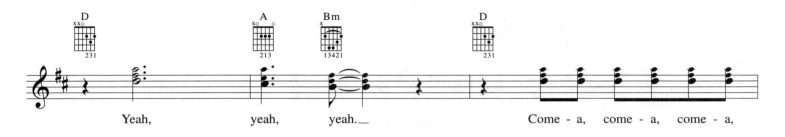
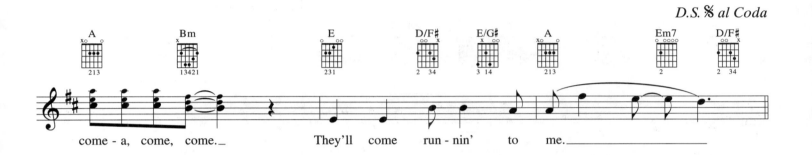
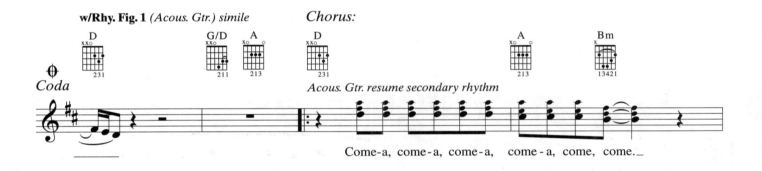
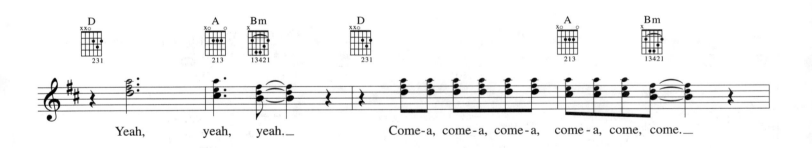
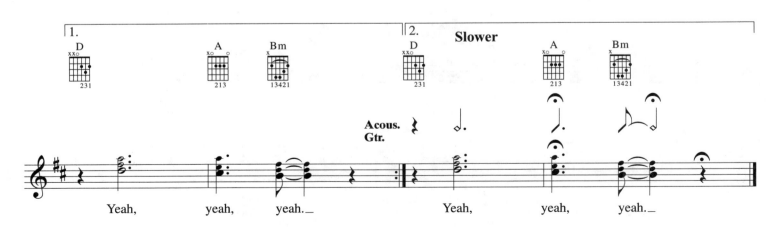

Handy Man - 4 - 4

HOTEL CALIFORNIA

Words and Music by
DON HENLEY, GLENN FREY
and DON FELDER

Gtr. 1 Chords:
Capo at 7th fret.

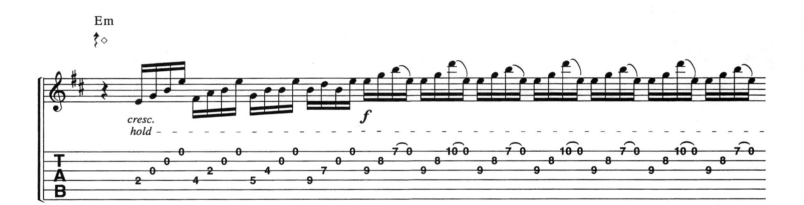

*Capo at 7th fret. All tab numbers shown as "7" are played as open strings.

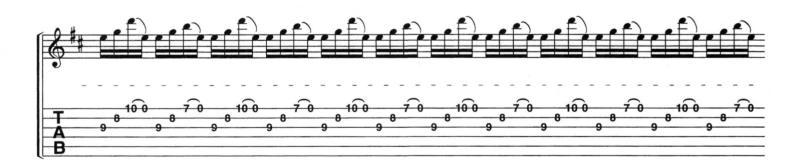

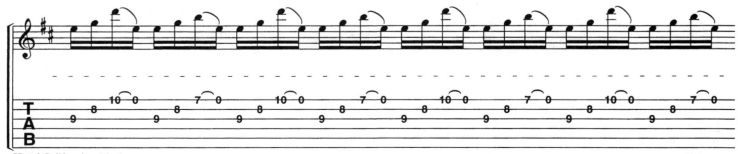

Hotel California - 16 - 1

© 1976 (Renewed) CASS COUNTY MUSIC, RED CLOUD MUSIC and FINGERS MUSIC
All Print Rights for CASS COUNTY MUSIC and RED CLOUD MUSIC Administered by WARNER-TAMERLANE PUBLSIHING CORP.
All Rights for FINGERS MUSIC Administered by WB MUSIC CORP.
All Rights Reserved

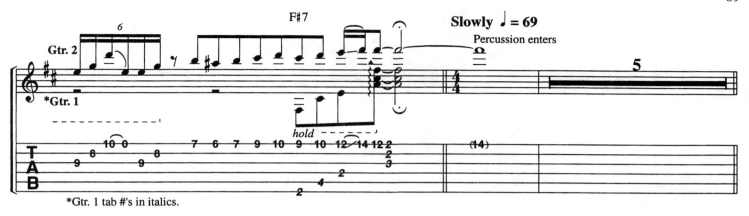
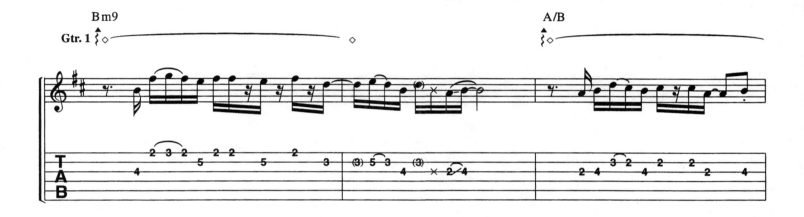
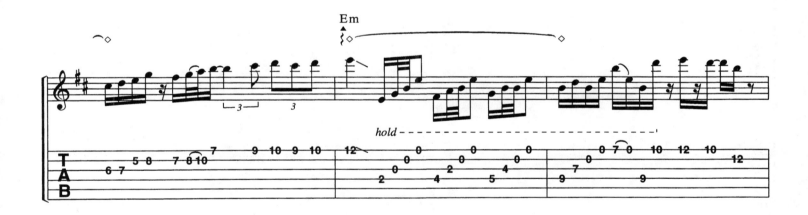

Hotel California - 16 - 2

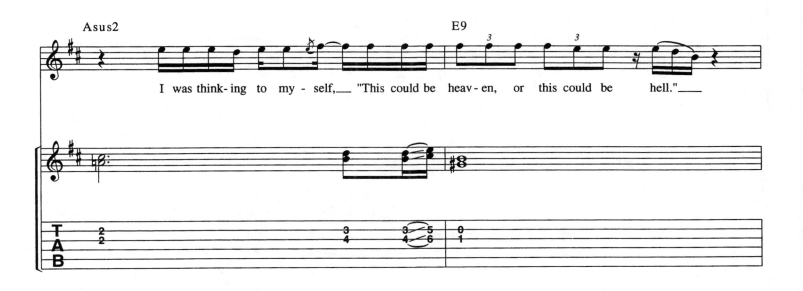
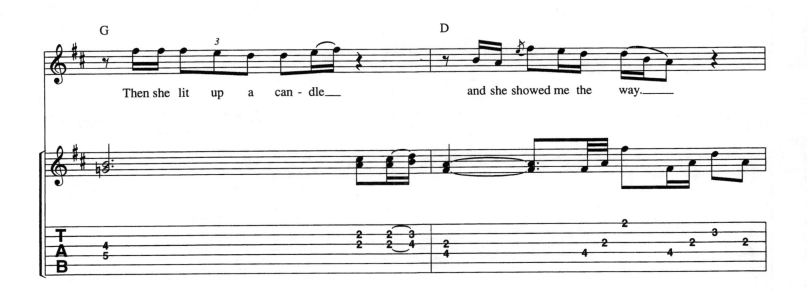

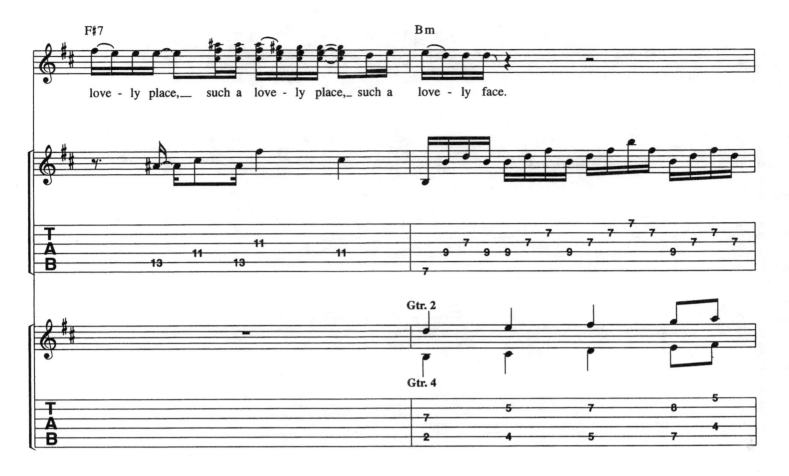

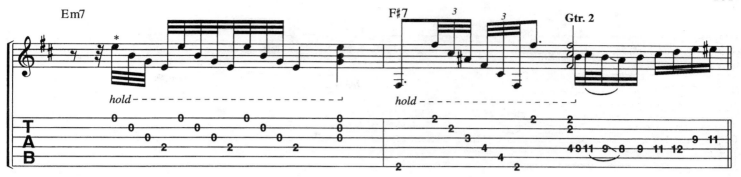

*"Roll" w/pick hand fingers

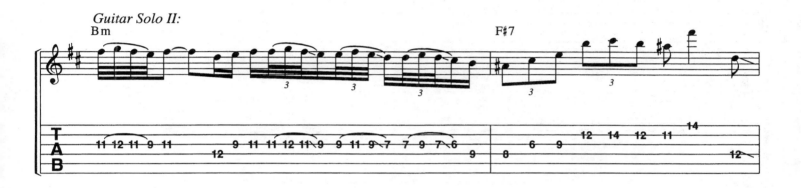

Guitar Solo II:

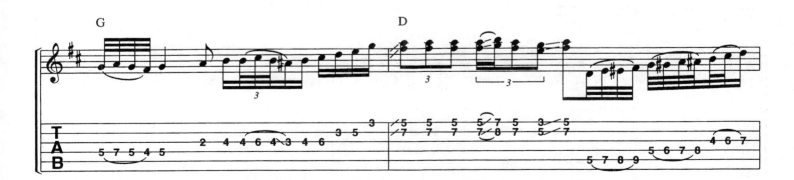

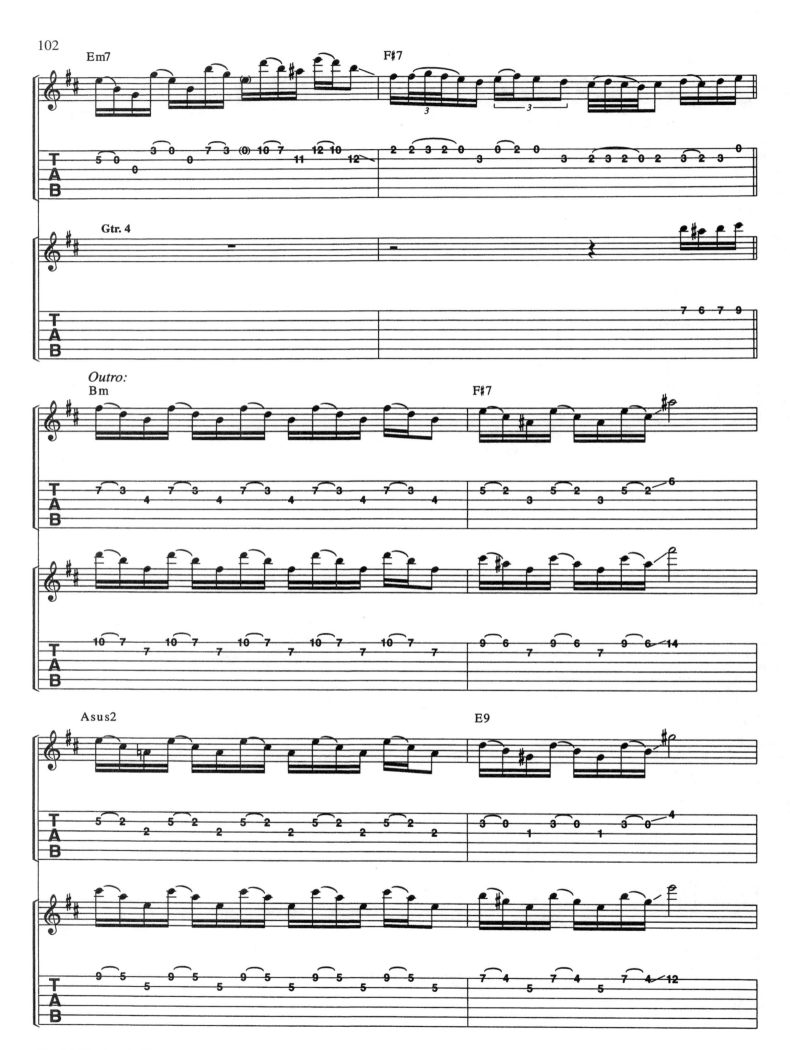

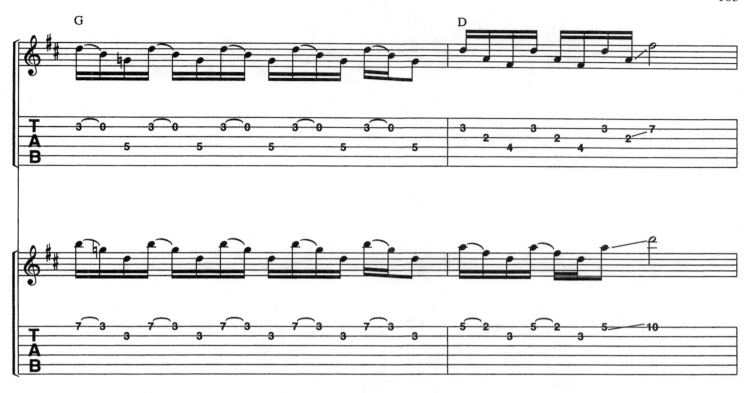
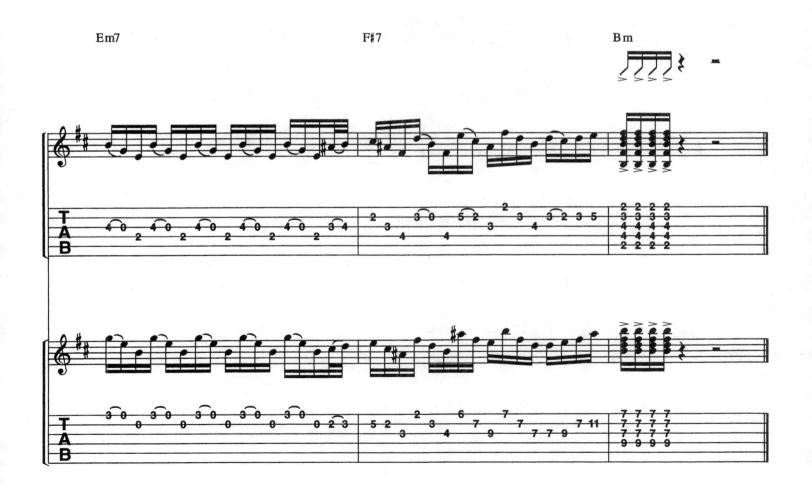

JESSE

Words and Music by
JANIS IAN

Moderately slow ♩ = 86

Intro:
w/strings

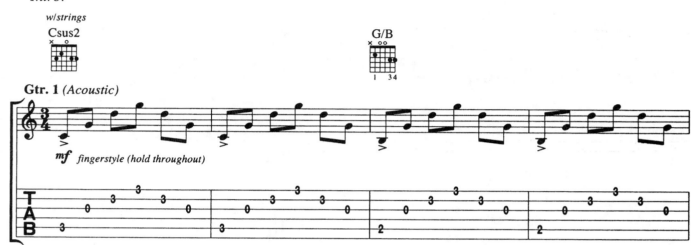

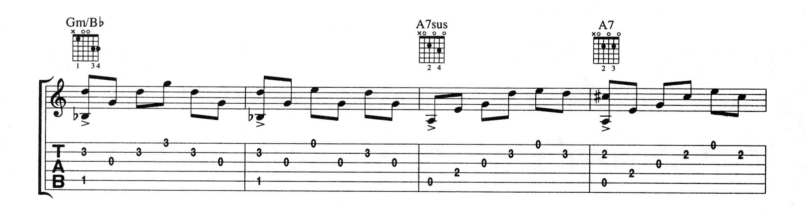

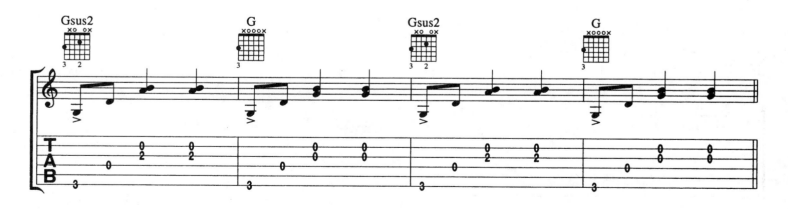

© 1972, 1973 (Copyrights Renewed) TAOSONGS TWO (BMI)
All Rights Reserved

Verse 2:
Jesse, the floors and the boards,
Recalling your steps,
And I remember too.
All the pictures are fading,
And shaded in grey,
But I still set a place
On the table at noon.
(To Chorus:)

Verse 3:
Jesse, the spread on the bed
Is like when you left
I've kept it up for you.
All the blues and the greens
Have been recently cleaned,
And it's seemingly new.
Hey, Jes me and you

Chorus 3:
We'll swallow the light on the stairs
We'll do up my hair and sleep unaware.
Hey, Jesse, I'm lonely
Come home.

LAYLA
(Unplugged)

Words and Music by
ERIC CLAPTON and
JIM GORDON

Intro
Moderately slow shuffle ♩.=92

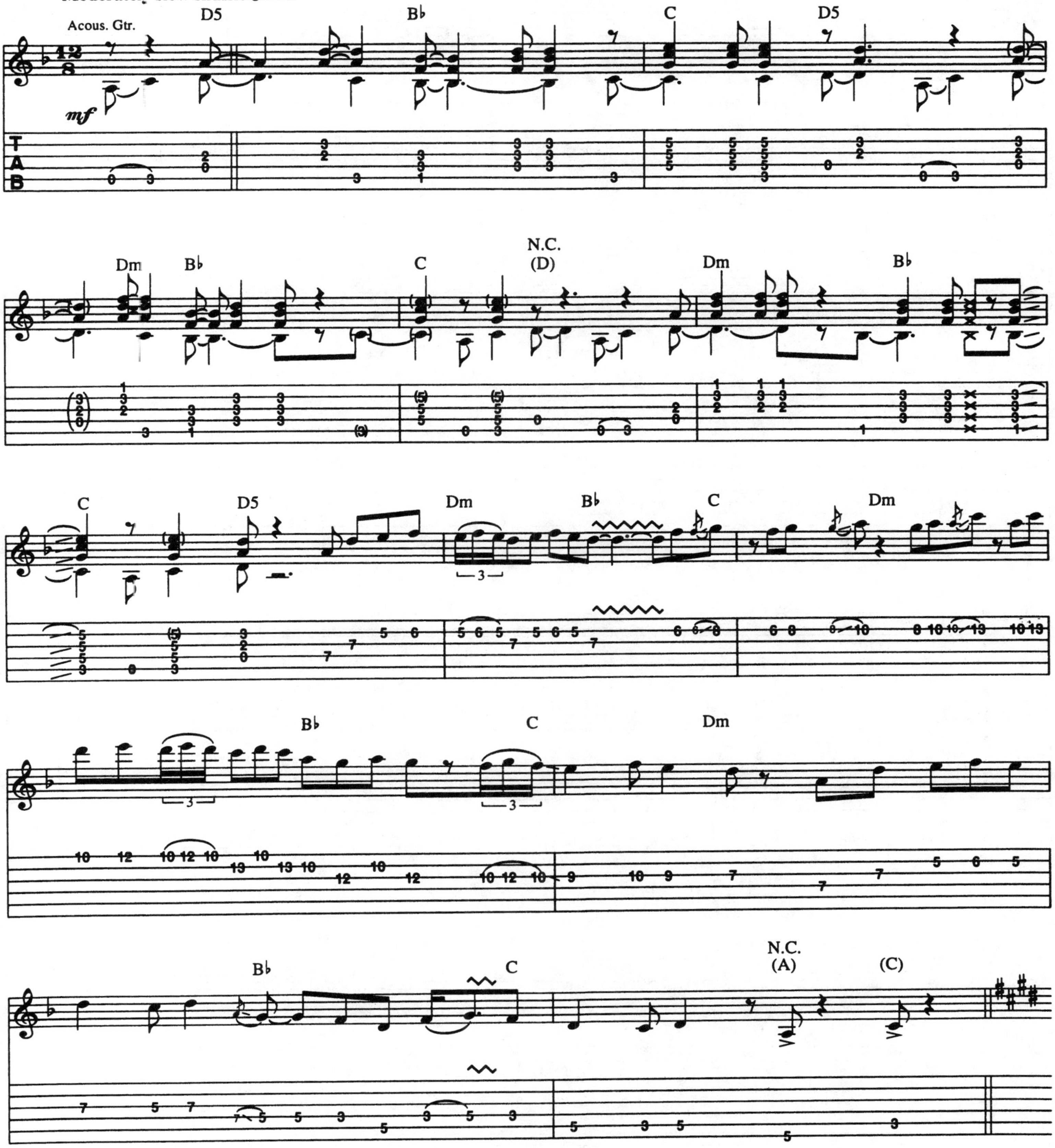

Lyin' Eyes - 9 - 2

she'll dress up all in lace___ and go in style.___
giv-en to a man with hands___ as cold as ice.___

3. So she___ You can't_

Chorus:

hide_____ your ly - in' eyes,___

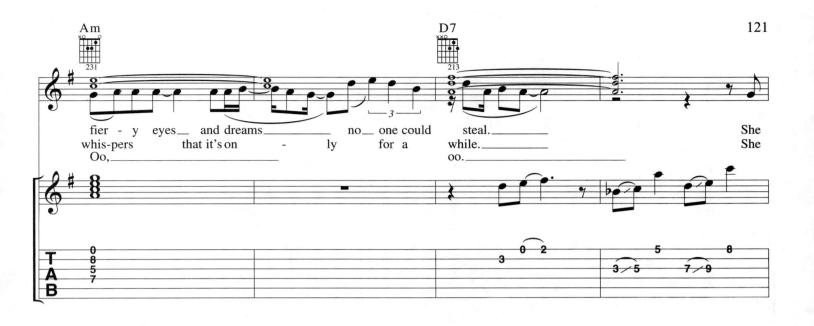
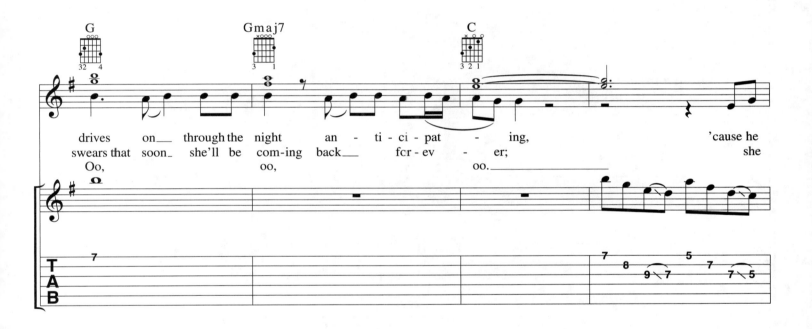

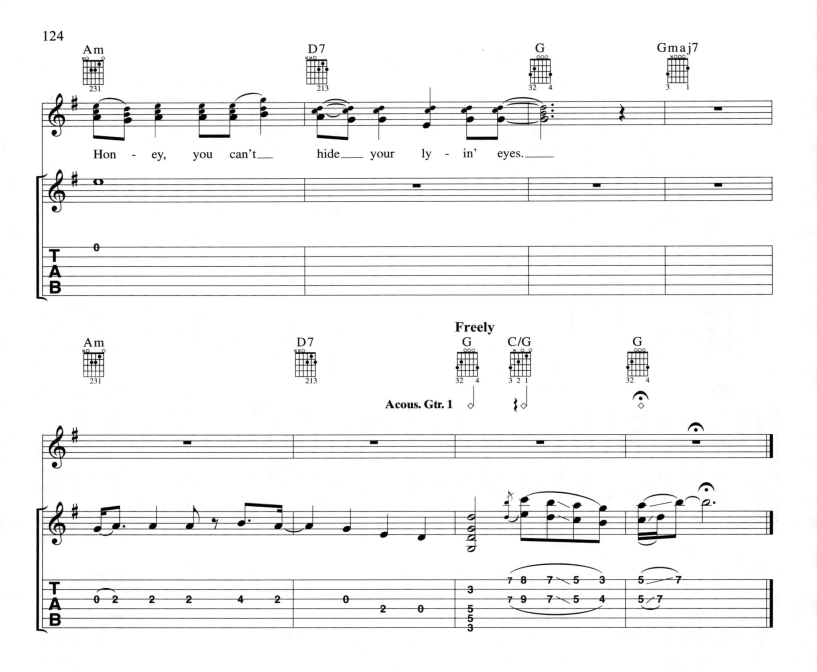

Verse 3:
So she tells him she must go out for the evening
To comfort an old friend who's feeling down.
But he knows where she's going as she's leaving.
She is headed for the cheating side of town.
(To Chorus:)

Verse 6:
She gets up and pours herself a strong one,
And stares out at the stars up in the sky.
Another night it's gonna be a long one,
She draws the shade and hangs her head to cry.

Verse 7:
She wonders how it ever got this crazy.
She thinks about a boy she knew in school.
Did she get tired or did she just get lazy?
She's so far gone she feels just like a fool.

Verse 8:
My, oh, my, you sure know how to arrange things,
You set it up so well, so carefully
Ain't it funny how your new life didn't change things,
You're still the same old girl you used to be.
(To Chorus:)

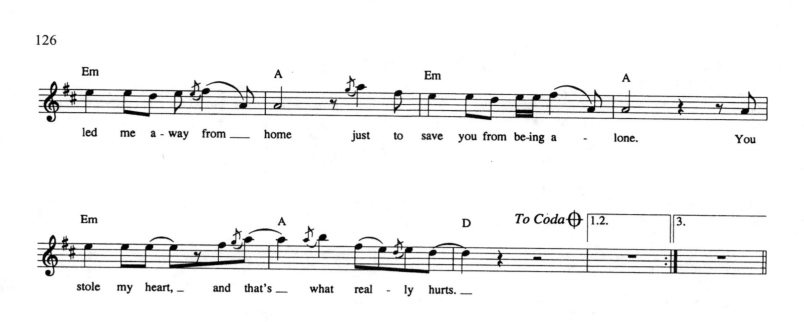

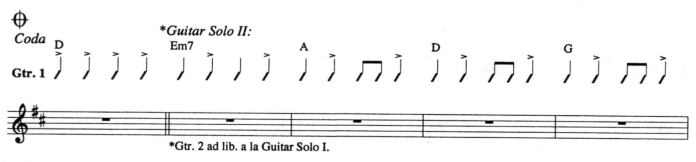

*Gtr. 2 ad lib. a la Guitar Solo I.

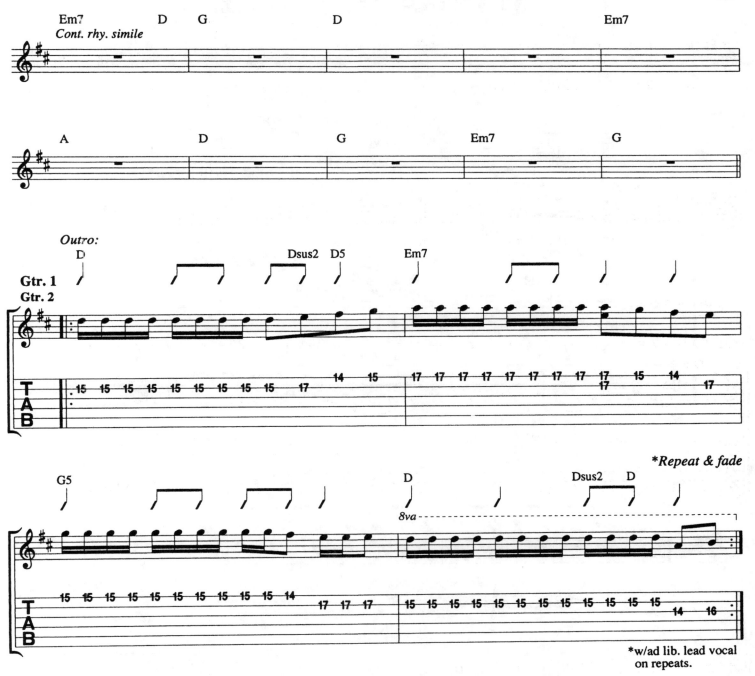

Verse 2:
The morning sun, when it's in your face,
Really shows your age.
But that don't worry me none,
In my eyes you're everything.
I laughed at all of your jokes,
My love you didn't need to coax.
Oh, Maggie, I couldn't have tried anymore.
You lead me away from home just to save
You from being alone.
You stole my soul, and that's a pain
I could live without.

Verse 3:
All I needed was a friend to lend
A guiding hand.
But you turned into a lover, and
Mother, what a lover, you wore me out.
All you did was wreck my bed,
And then the morning kicked me in the head.
Oh, Maggie, I couldn't have tried anymore.
You lead me away from home 'cause you
Didn't want to be alone.
You stole my heart, I couldn't leave you if I tried.
(To Guitar Solo I:)

Verse 4:
I suppose I could collect my books
And get on back to school.
Or steal my daddy's cue, and make a living out of playing pool.
Or find myself a rock and roll band that needs a helping hand.
Oh Maggie, I wish I'd never seen your face.
You made a first-class fool out of me,
But I'm as blind as a fool can be.
You stole my heart, but I love you anyway.
(To Guitar Solo II:)

MARGARITAVILLE

Words and Music by
JIMMY BUFFETT

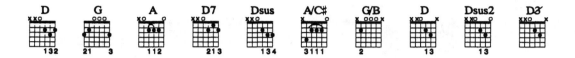
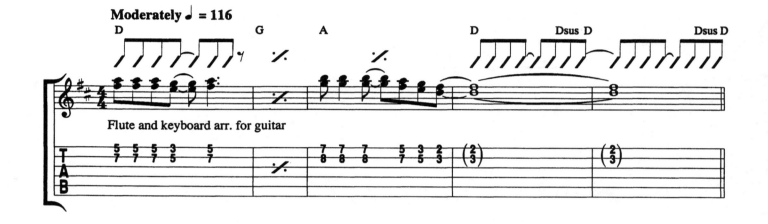

© 1977 (Renewed) CORAL REEFER MUSIC
All Rights Reserved

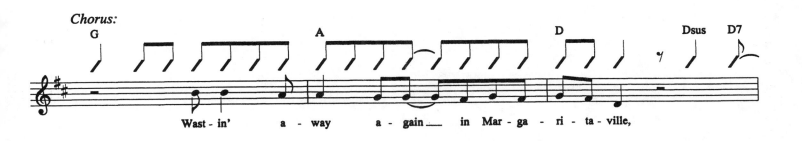

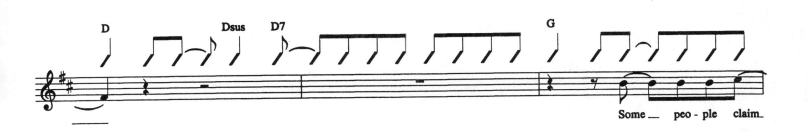
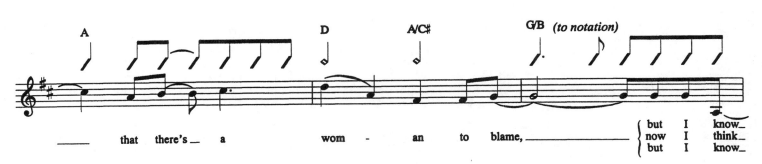

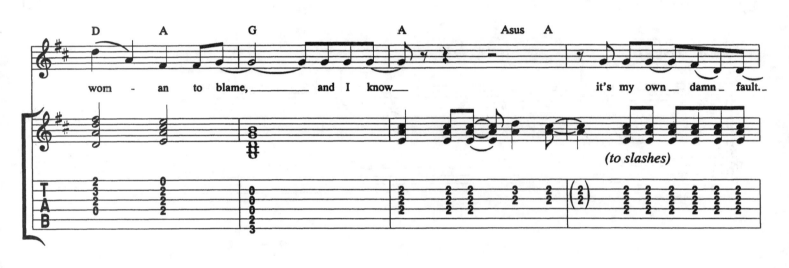

Verse 3:

I blew out my flip-flop,
Stepped on a pop top;
Cut my heel, had to cruise on back home.
But there's booze in the blender,
And soon it will render
That frozen concoction that helps me hang on.

MEXICO

Words and Music by
JAMES TAYLOR

*Capo at 2nd fret. Two acoustic guitars arranged as one.

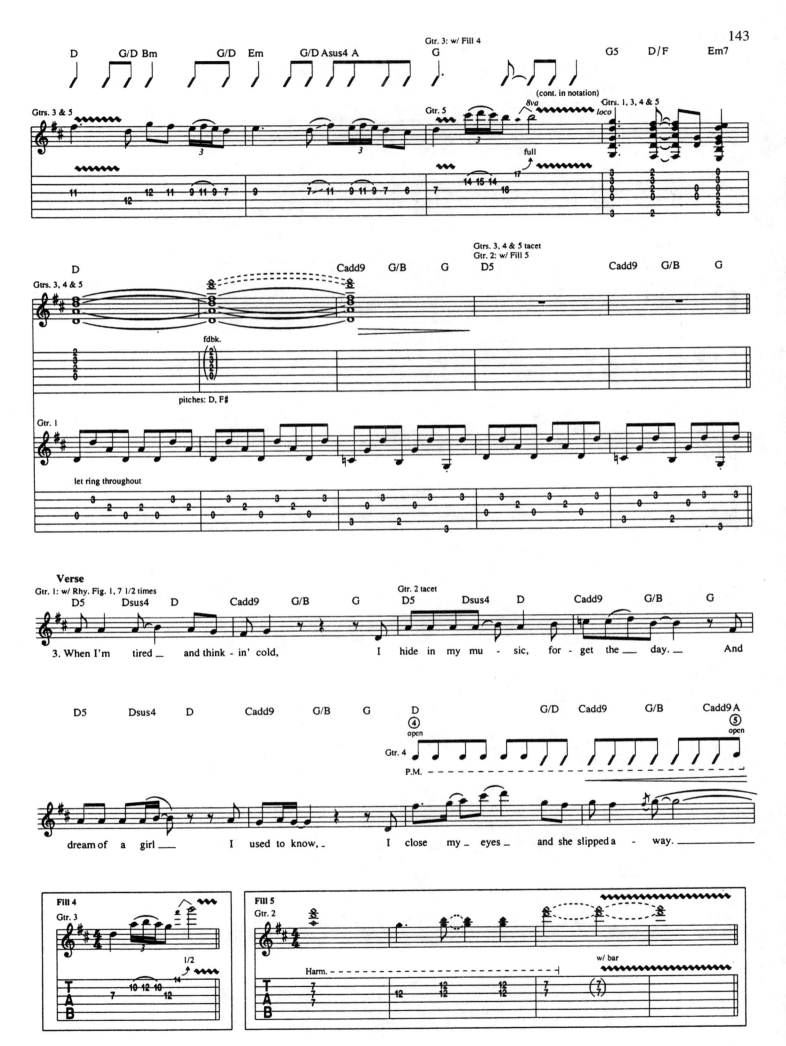

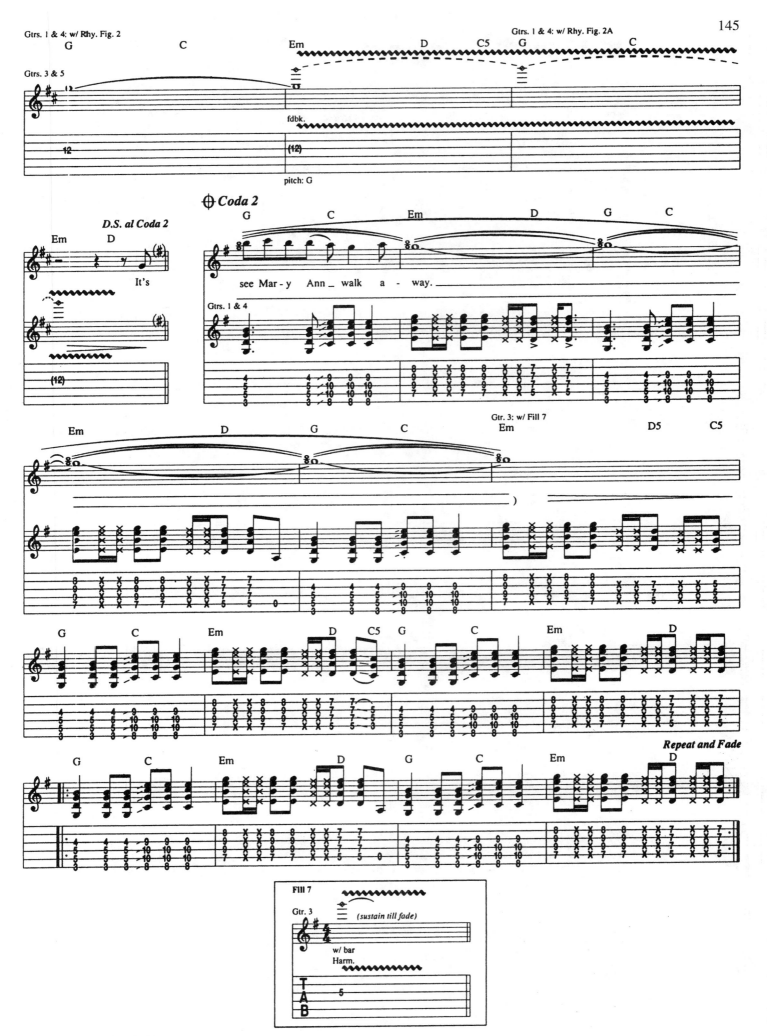

147

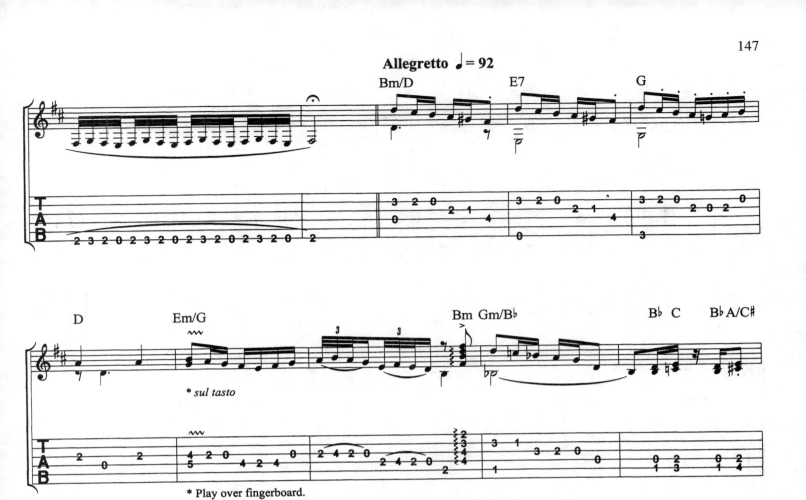

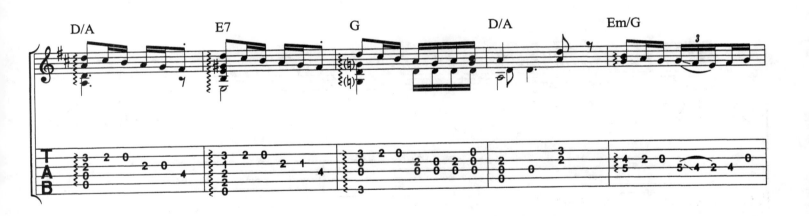

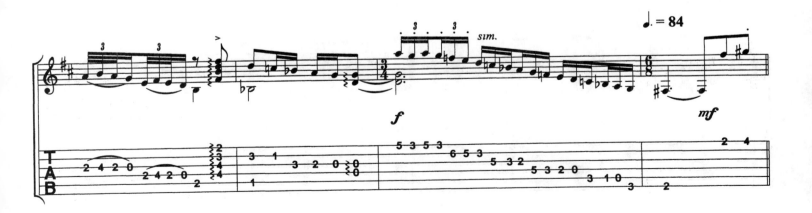

Mood for a Day - 4 - 4

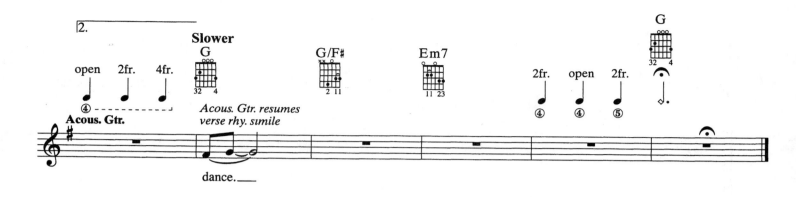

Verse 2:
I met him in a cell in New Orleans.
I was down and out.
He looked to me to be
The eyes of age
As he spoke right out.
He talked of life.
He talked of life.
He laughed, clicked his heels and stepped.

Verse 3:
He said his name, "Bojangles," and he danced a lick
Across the cell.
He grabbed his pants and spread his stance,
Woah, he jumped so high
And then he clicked his heels.
He let go a laugh.
He let go a laugh,
Shook back his clothes all around.

Verse 4:
He danced for those in minstrel shows and county fairs
Throughout the South.
He spoke through tears of fifteen years,
How his dog and him
Travelled about.
The dog up and died.
He up and died.
After twenty years, he still grieves.

Verse 5:
He said, "I've danced now
At every chance in honky tonk
For drinks and tips.
But most the time was spent behind these county bars
'Cause I drinks a bit."
He shook his head.
And as he shook his head,
I heard someone ask him, "Please, please"…

OPERATOR
(THAT'S NOT THE WAY IT FEELS)

Words and Music by
JIM CROCE

*Capo at 5th fret.
**Chords in parenthesis are capo chords for Guitar 2 only.

© 1972 DENJAC MUSIC COMPANY
© Renewed 2000 and Assigned to CROCE PUBLISHING in the U.S.A.
All Rights outside the U.S.A. Administered by DENJAC MUSIC COMPANY
All Rights Reserved

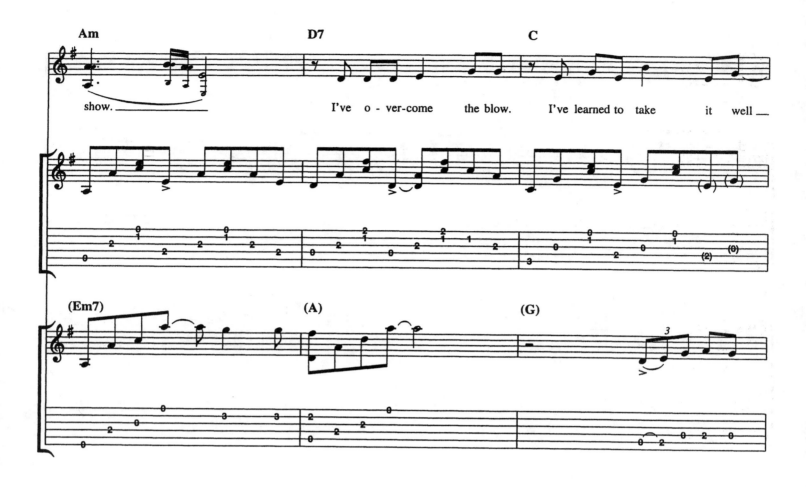
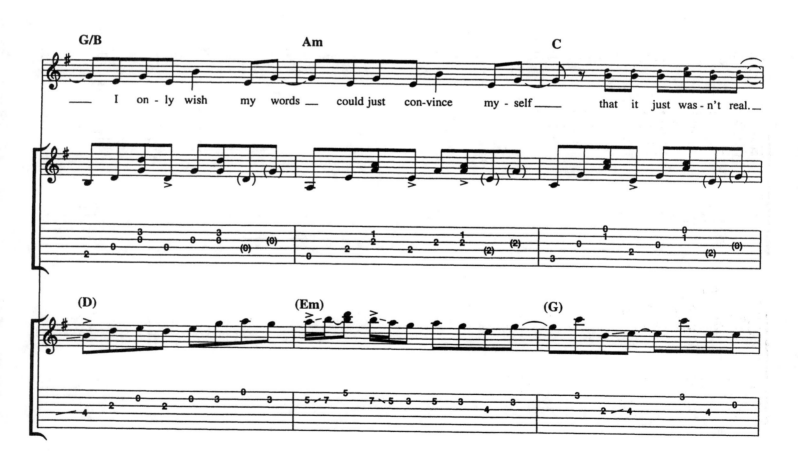

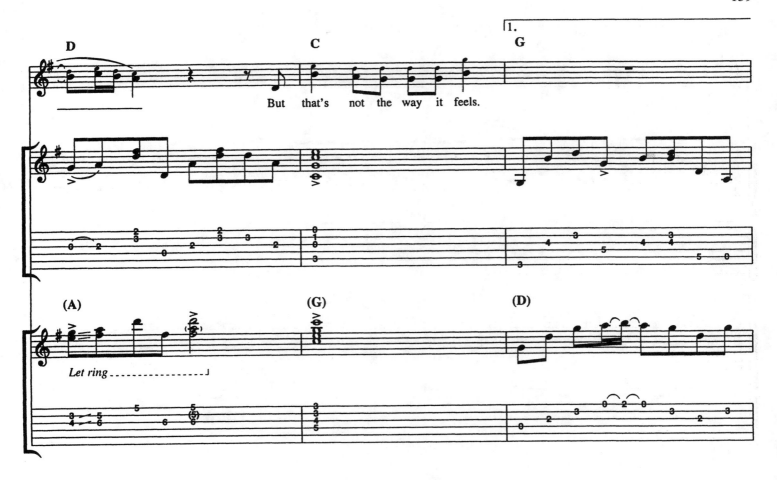
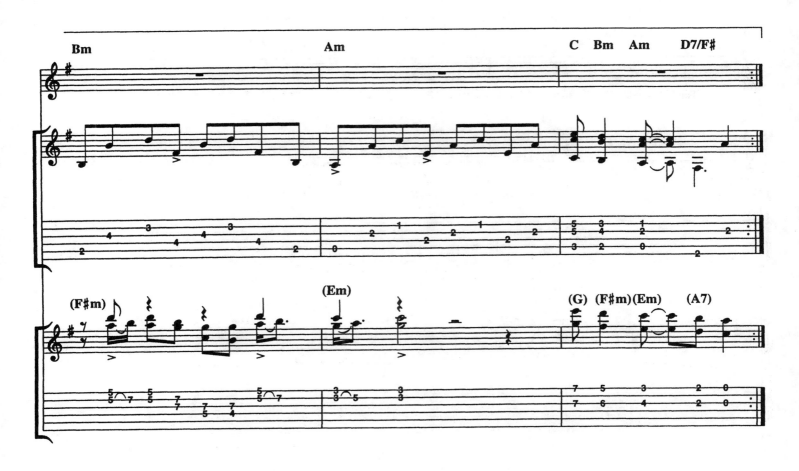

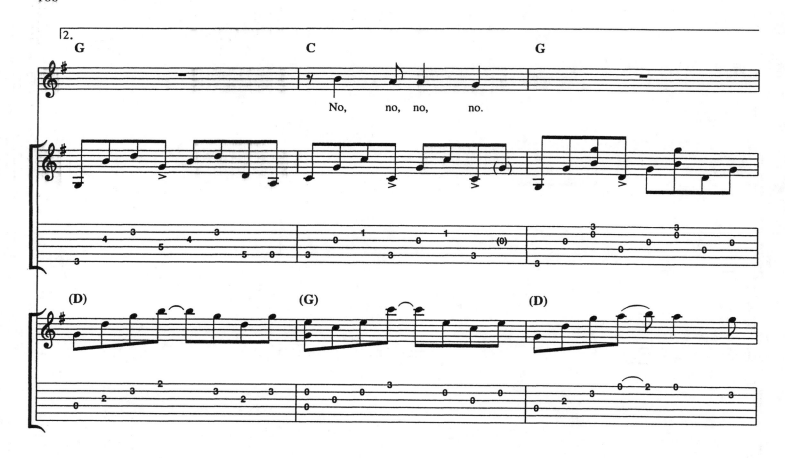

Operator (That's Not the Way It Feels) - 9 - 8

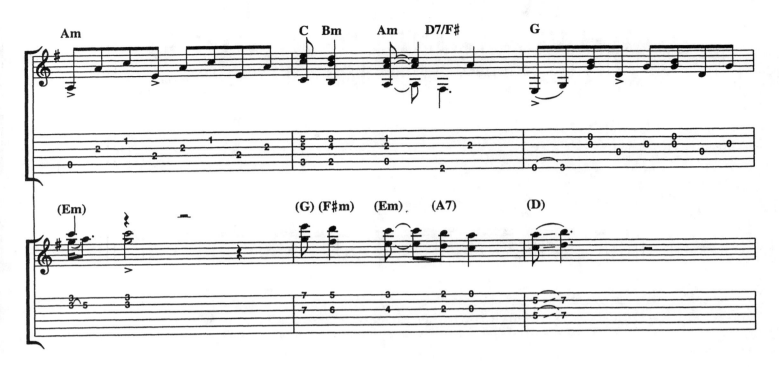
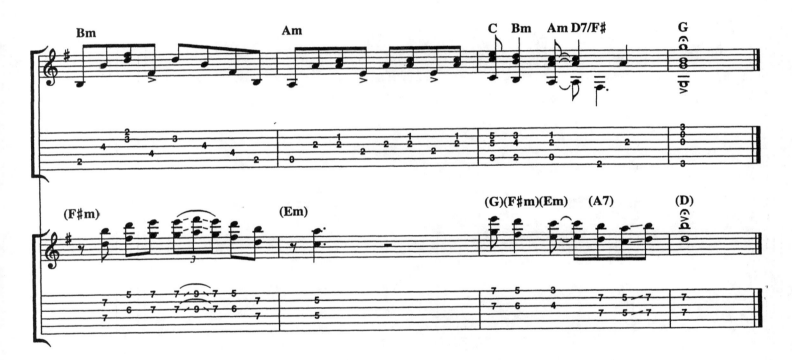

Additional lyrics

2. Operator, oh could you help me place this call?
   'Cause I can't read the number that you just gave me.
   There's something in my eyes,
   You know it happens every time;
   I think about the love that I thought would save me.

   (To Chorus:)

3. Operator, oh let's forget about this call.
   (There's) no one there I really wanted to talk to.
   Thank you for your time.
   Oh, you've been so much more than kind
   You can keep your dime.

   (To Chorus:)

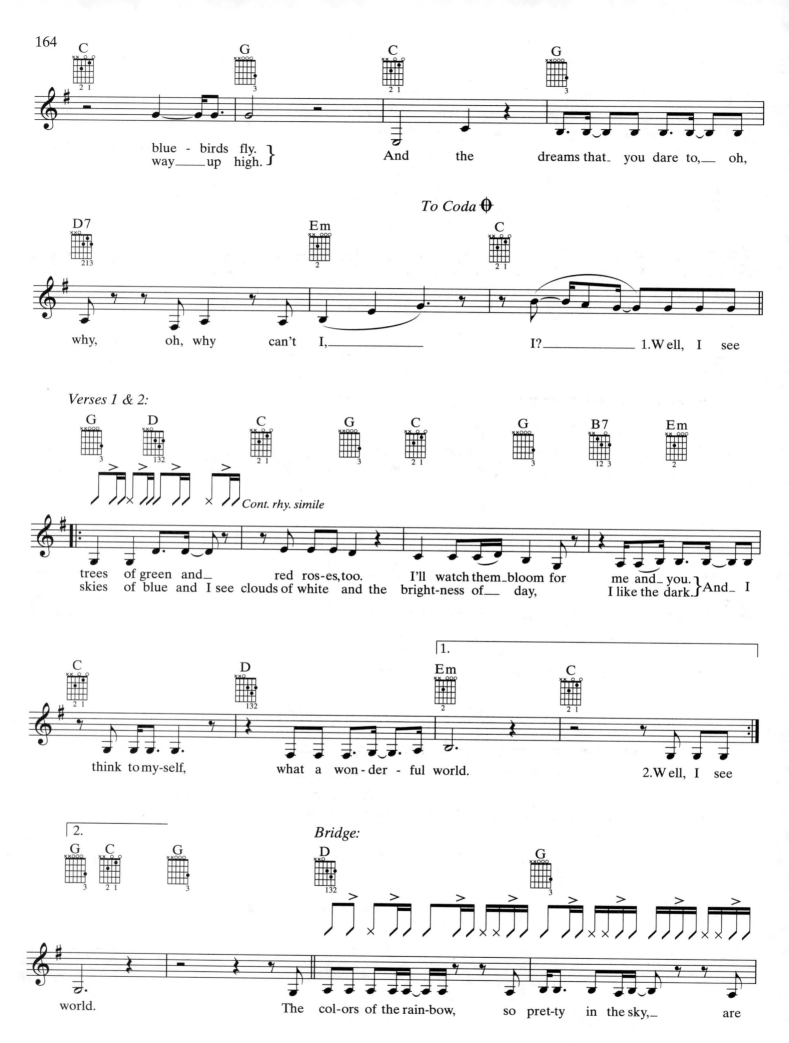

PEACEFUL EASY FEELING

Moderately fast ♩ = 140

Words and Music by
JACK TEMPCHIN

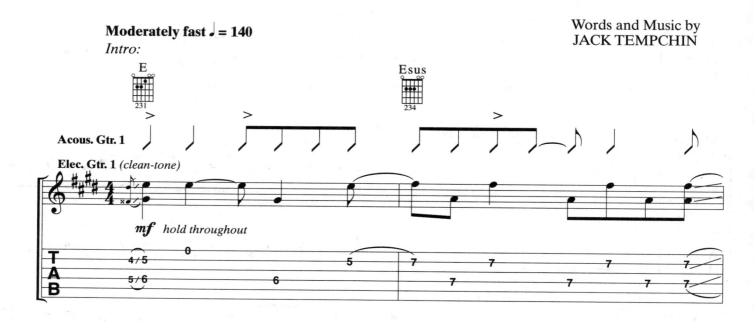

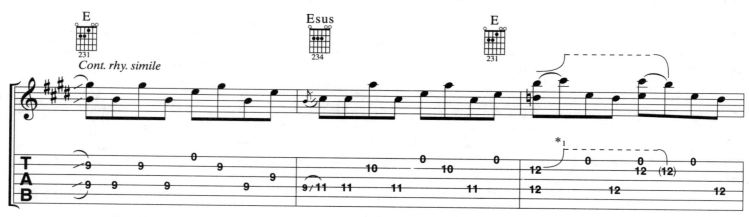

* On the recording, all bends on the 2nd string are played by using a "B bender." You can duplicate this effect by using hammer ons and pull offs to replace the bends.

© 1972 (Renewed) WB MUSIC CORP. and JAZZ BIRD MUSIC
All Rights Administered by WB MUSIC CORP.
All Rights Reserved

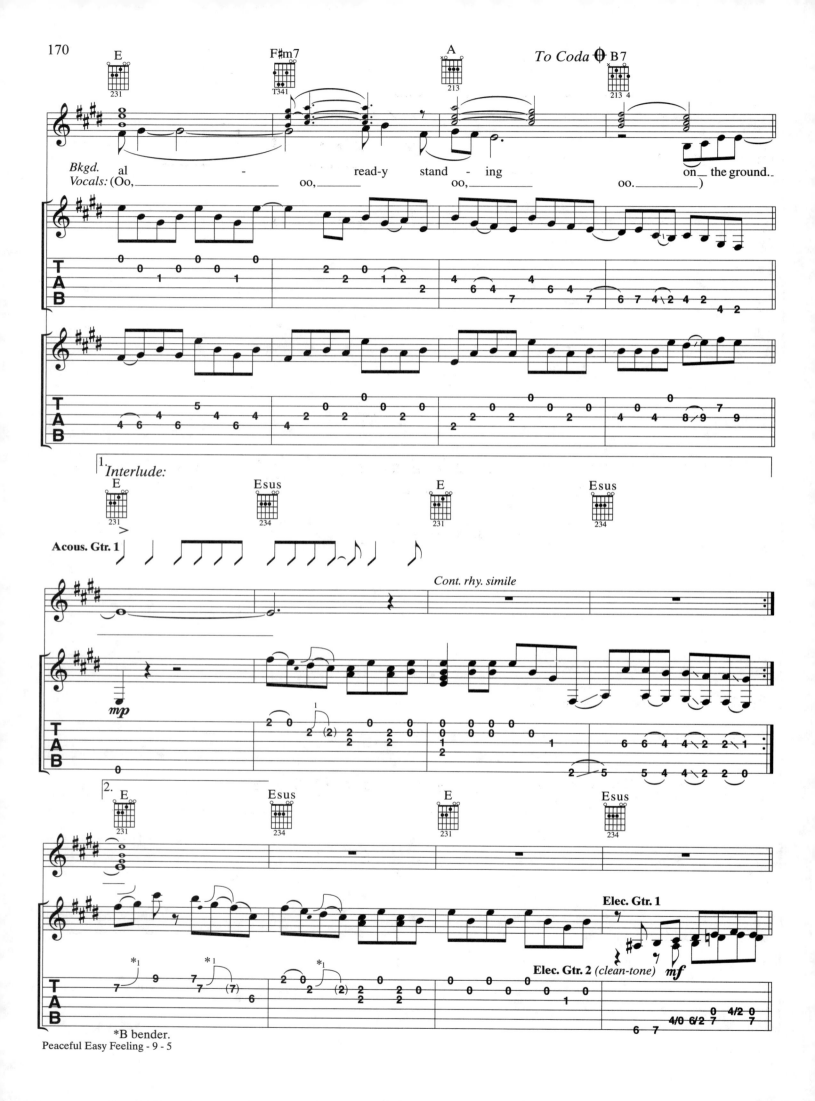

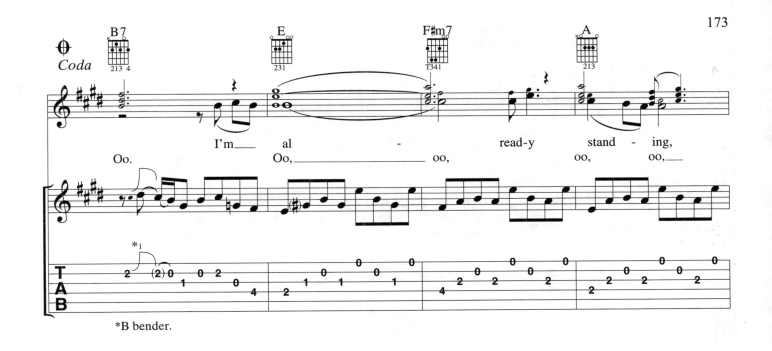
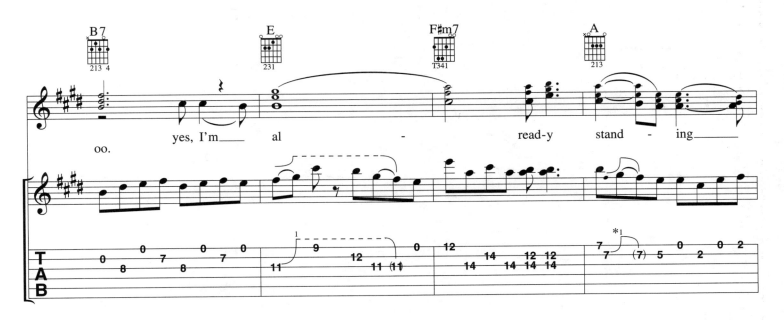

Verse 3:
I got this feeling I may know you
As a lover and a friend.
But this voice keeps whispering in my other ear,
Tells me I may never see you again.
(To Chorus:)

ROCKY MOUNTAIN HIGH

Tune Gtr. to Drop D
w/capo at 2nd fret:
⑥ = E ③ = G
⑤ = A ② = B
④ = D ① = E

Words and Music by
JOHN DENVER and Mike TAYLOR

Moderately ♩ = 66

Intro:

Cont. in slashes

Verse:

Cont. rhy. simile

1. He was born in the sum-
2.–5. *See additional lyrics*

-mer of his twen-ty-sev-enth year, com-in' home to a

place he'd nev-er been be-fore. He left yes-ter-day be-hind

him, you might say he was born a-gain. You might say he found the key

© 1972 Cherry Lane Music Publishing Company, Inc. and DreamWorks Songs
© Renewed 2000 and Assigned in the U.S. to Jesse Belle Denver, Anna Kate Deutschendorf, Zachary Deutschendorf,
Cherry Lane Music Publishing Company, Inc. and DreamWorks Songs
All Rights for Jesse Belle Denver Administered by WB Music Corp.
All Rights for Anna Kate Deutschendorf and Zachary Deutschendorf Administered by Cherry Lane Music Publishing Company, Inc.
All Rights for the world excluding the U.S. Controlled by Cherry Lane Music Publishing Company, Inc. and DreamWorks Songs
All Rights Reserved

Verse 2:
When he first came to the mountains his life was far away,
On the road and hangin' by a song.
But the string's already broken and he doesn't really care.
It keeps changin' fast, and it don't last for long.
(To Chorus 1:)

Verse 3:
He climbed cathedral mountains, he saw silver clouds below.
He saw everything as far as you can see.
And they say that he got crazy once and he tried to touch the sun,
And he lost a friend but kept his memory.

Verse 4:
Now he walks in quiet solitude the forests and the streams,
Seeking grace in every step he takes.
His sight has turned inside himself to try and understand
The serenity of a clear blue mountain lake.

Chorus 2:
And the Colorado Rocky Mountain high,
I've seen it rainin' fire in the sky.
You can talk to God and listen to the casual reply.
Rocky Mountain high. (In Colorado.)
Rocky Mountain high. (In Colorado.)

Verse 5:
Now his life is full of wonder but his heart still knows some fear
Of a simple thing he cannot comprehend.
Why they try to tear the mountains down to bring in a couple more,
More people, more scars upon the land.

Chorus 3:
And the Colorado Rocky Mountain high,
I've seen it rainin' fire in the sky.
I know he'd be a poorer man if he never saw an eagle fly.
Rocky Mountain high.

Chorus 4:
It's a Colorado Rocky Mountain high.
I've seen it rainin' fire in the sky.
Friends around the campfire and everybody's high.
Rock Mountain high. (In Colorado.)

THE RIVER

Words and Music by
BRUCE SPRINGSTEEN

© 1979, 1981 BRUCE SPRINGSTEEN (ASCAP)
All Rights Reserved

Verse 3:
I got a job working construction for the Johnstown Company,
But lately there ain't been much work on account of the economy.
Now all them things that seemed so important,
Well, mister, they vanished right into the air.
Now I just act like I don't remember.
Mary acts like she don't care.

Verse 4:
But I remember us riding in my brother's car,
Her body tan and wet down at the reservoir.
At night, on them banks, I'd lie awake and pull her close
Just to feel each breath she'd take.
Now those memories come back to haunt me,
They haunt me like a curse.
Is a dream a lie if it don't come true,
Or is it something worse that sends me?
(To Chorus:)

Chorus:
Down to the river, though I know the river is dry,
That sends me down to the river tonight.
(To Coda)

SCARBOROUGH FAIR/CANTICLE

*Acous. Gtr. Capo VII

Arrangement and original counter melody by
PAUL SIMON and ARTHUR GARFUNKEL

Moderately ♩. = 42

*Recording sounds three and a half steps higher than written.

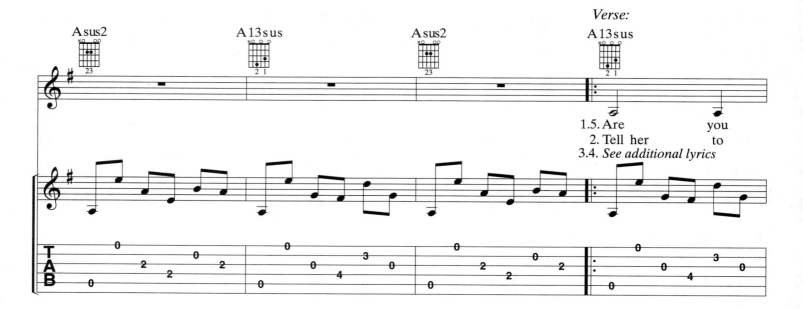

1.5. Are you
2. Tell her to
3.4. *See additional lyrics*

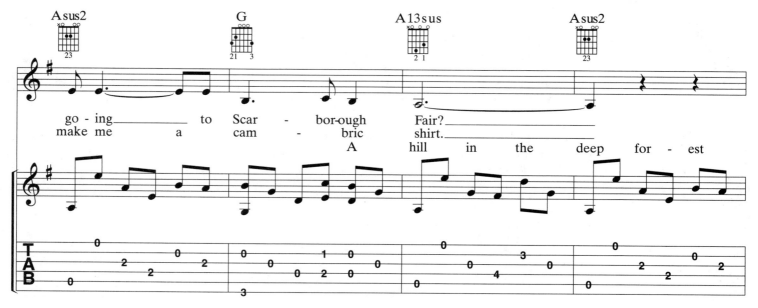

go-ing to Scar-bor-ough Fair?
make me a cam-bric shirt.
A hill in the deep for-est

© 1966 PAUL SIMON (BMI)
International Copyright Secured   All Rights Reserved
Reprinted by Permission of MUSIC SALES CORPORATION (ASCAP)

Verse 3:
Tell her to find me an acre of land.
On the side of a hill a sprinkling of leaves.
Parsely, sage, rosemary and thyme.
Washes the grave with silvery tears.
Between the salt water and the sea strand.
A soldier cleans and polishes a gun.
Then she'll be a true love of mine.
Sleeps unaware of the clarion call.

Verse 4:
Tell her to reap it in a sickle of leather.
War bellows blazing in scarlet battalions.
Parsley, sage, rosemary and thyme.
Generals order their soldiers to kill.
And gather it all in a bunch of heather.
And to fight for a cause they've long ago forgotten.
Then she'll be a true love of mine.

SHOWER THE PEOPLE

Words and Music by
JAMES TAYLOR

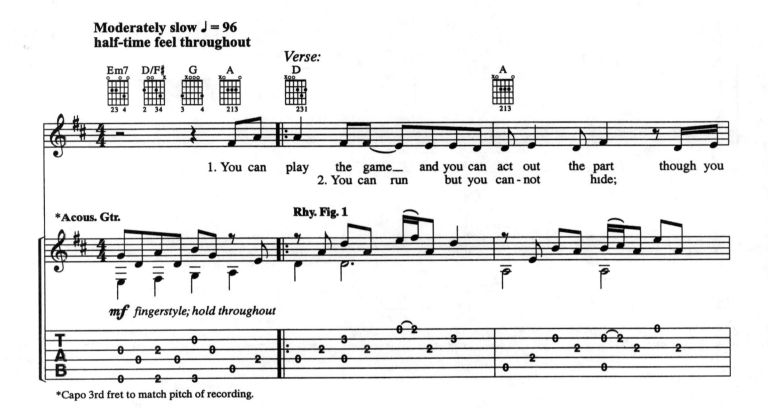

© 1975 (Renewed) COUNTRY ROAD MUSIC, INC.
All Rights Reserved

Outro (vocal ad lib.):
They say in every life,
They say the rain must fall.
Just like a pouring rain,
Make it rain.
Love is sunshine.

SON OF A SON OF A SAILOR

Words and Music by
JIMMY BUFFETT

Son of a Son of a Sailor - 4 - 1

© 1978 CORAL REEFER MUSIC and OUTER BANKS MUSIC
All Rights Administered by CORAL REEFER MUSIC
All Rights Reserved

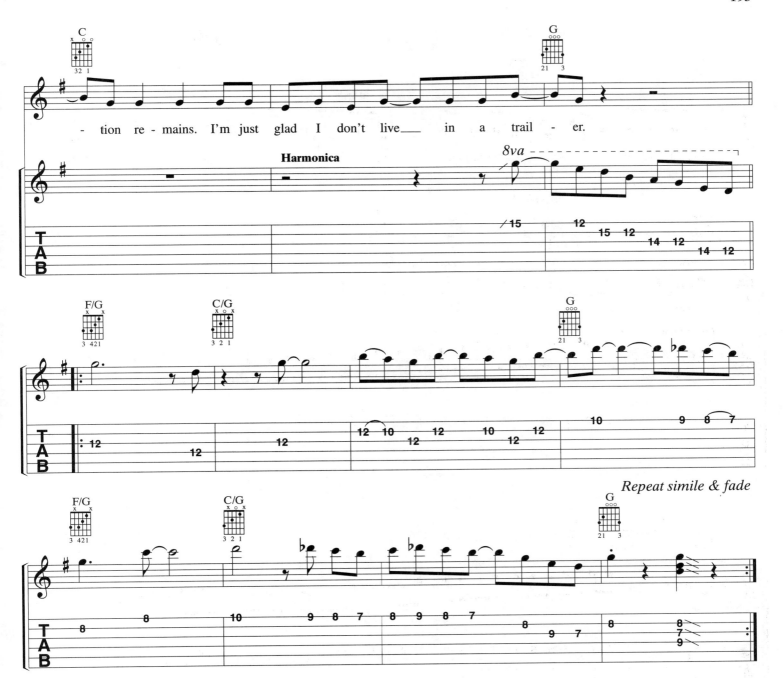

Verse 3:
Now away in the near future,
South-east of disorder,
You can shake the hand of the mango man
As he greets you at the border.

Verse 4:
And the lady she hails from Trinidad;
Island of the spices.
Salt for your meat, and cinnamon sweet,
And the rum is for all your good vices.

Chorus 2:
Haul the sheet in as we ride on the wind
That our fore-fathers harnessed before us.
Hear the bells ring as the tide rigging sings.
It's a son of a gun of a chorus.

Verse 5:
Where it all ends I can't fathom, my friends.
If I knew, I might toss out my anchor.
So I'll cruise along always searchin' for songs,
Not a lawyer, a thief or a banker.
(To Chorus 3:)

STREETS OF PHILADELPHIA

Words and Music by
BRUCE SPRINGSTEEN

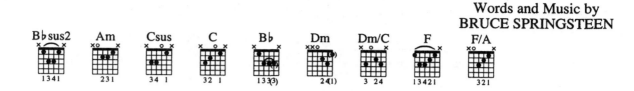

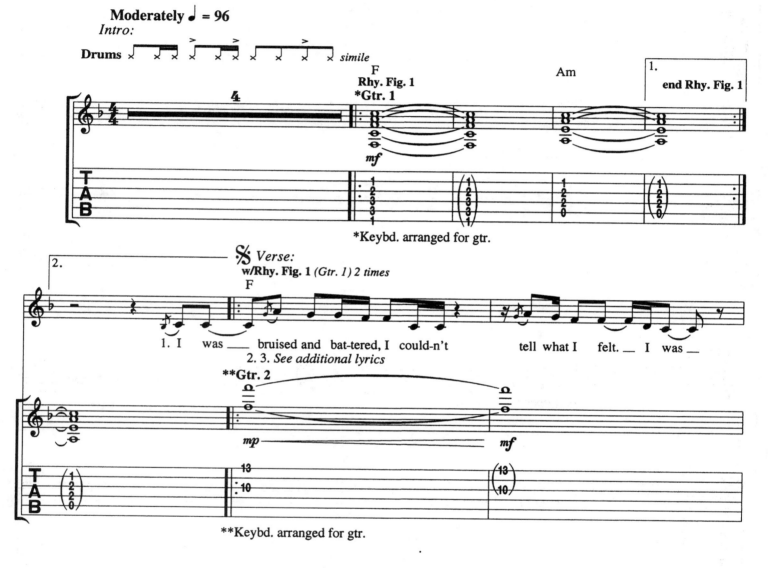

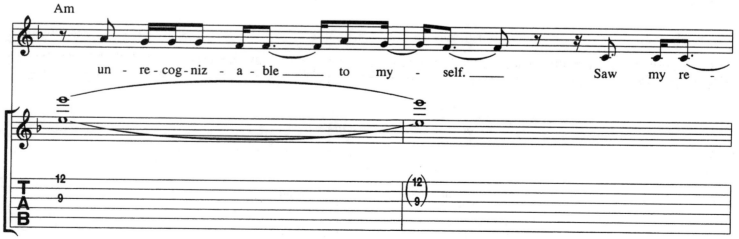

198

Streets of Philadelphia – 4 – 3

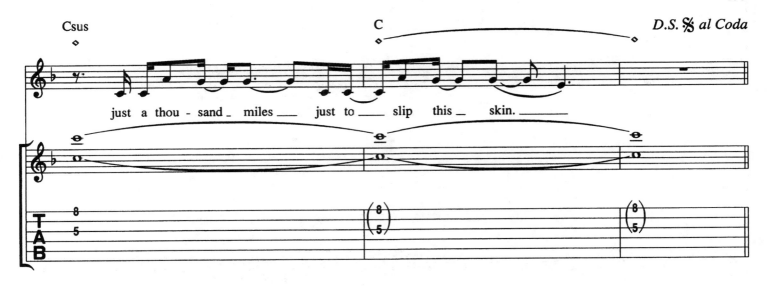

Verse 2:
I walked the avenue till my legs felt like stone,
I heard the voices of friends vanished and gone.
At night, I could hear the blood in my veins,
Black and whispering as the rain
On the streets of Philadelphia...
(To Chorus:)

Verse 3:
The night has fallen, I'm lyin' awake,
I can feel myself fading away.
So receive me, brother, with your faithless kiss
Or will we leave each other alone like this
On the streets of Philadelphia...
(To Chorus:)

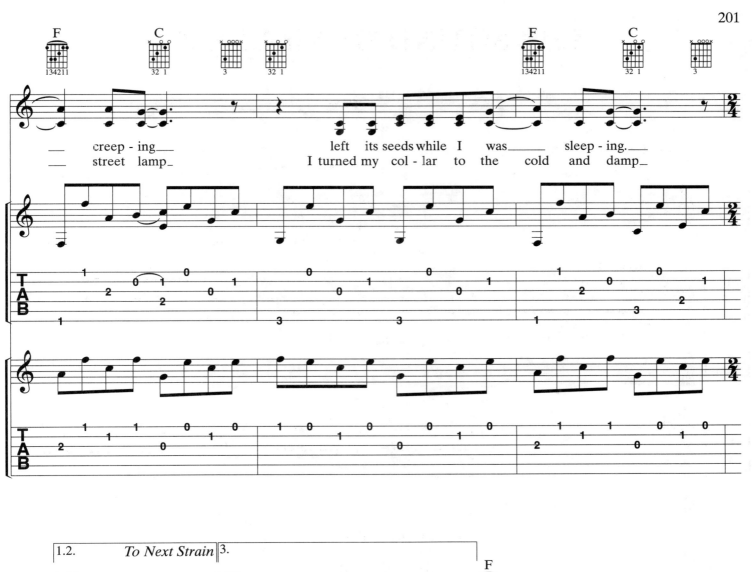
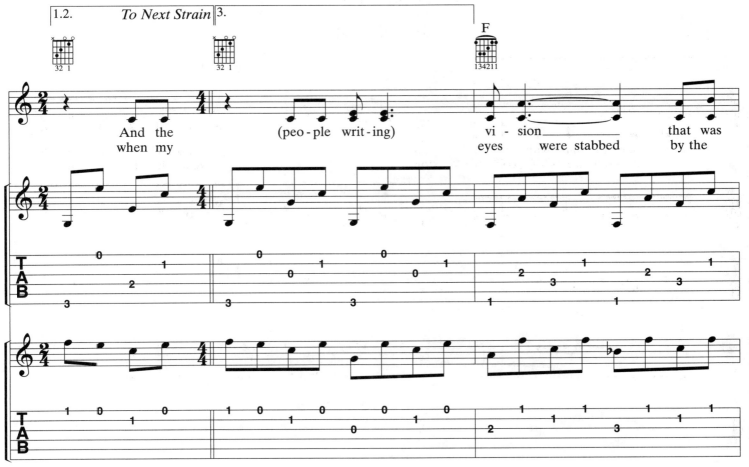

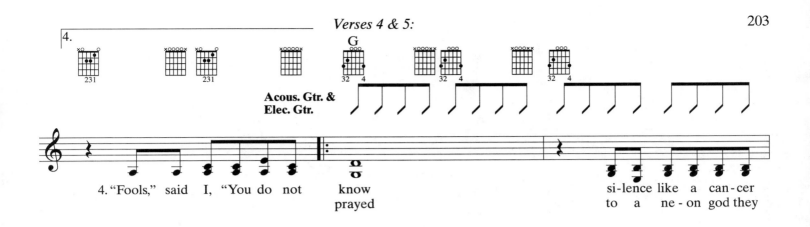

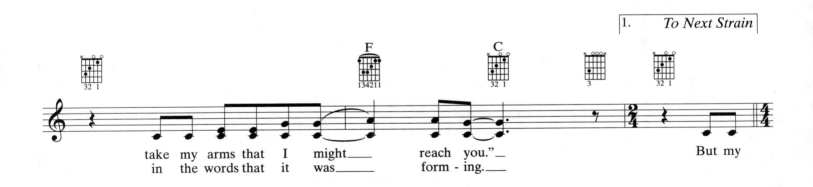

Verse 3:
And in the naked light I saw
Ten thousand people, maybe more.
People talking without speaking,
People hearing without listening.
People writing songs that voices never share
And no one dared
Disturb the sound of silence.
(To Verse 4:)

STILL CRAZY AFTER ALL THESE YEARS

Words and Music by
PAUL SIMON

© 1974 Paul Simon (BMI)
International Copyright Secured   All Rights Reserved
Reprinted by Permission of Music Sales Corporation (ASCAP)

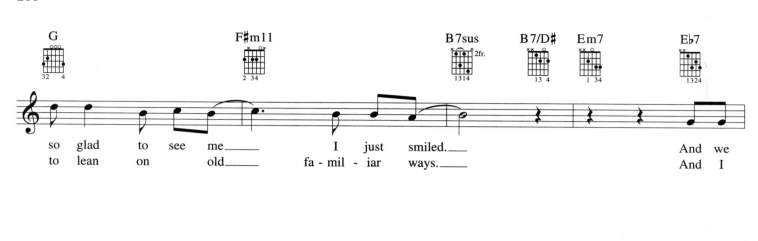
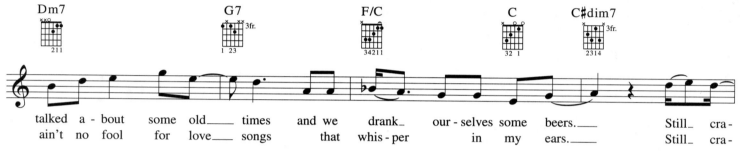
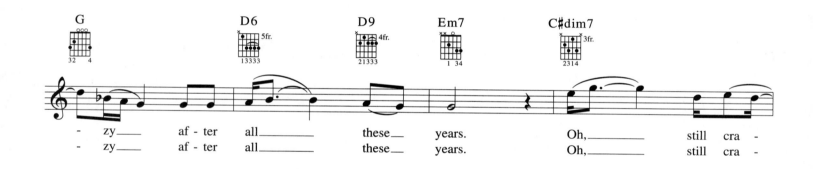
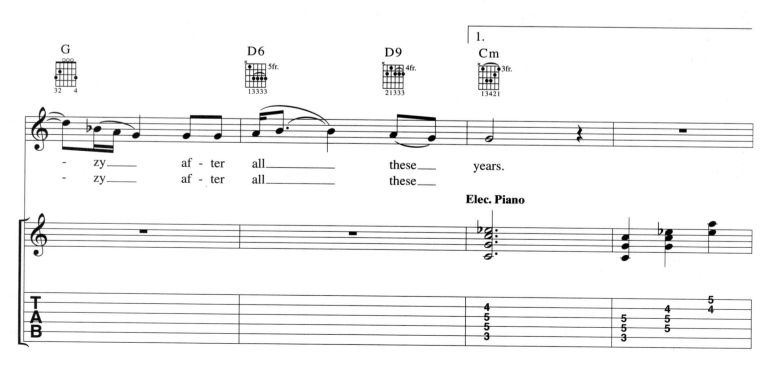

Still Crazy After All These Years - 5 - 2

SUNDOWN

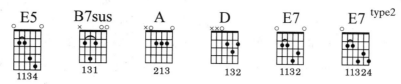

Words and Music by
GORDON LIGHTFOOT

All gtrs. capo 2nd fret.

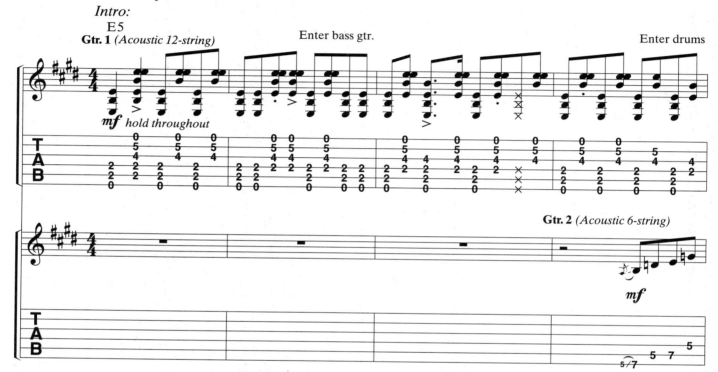

© 1973 MOOSE MUSIC LTD. (Renewed)
All Rights Reserved

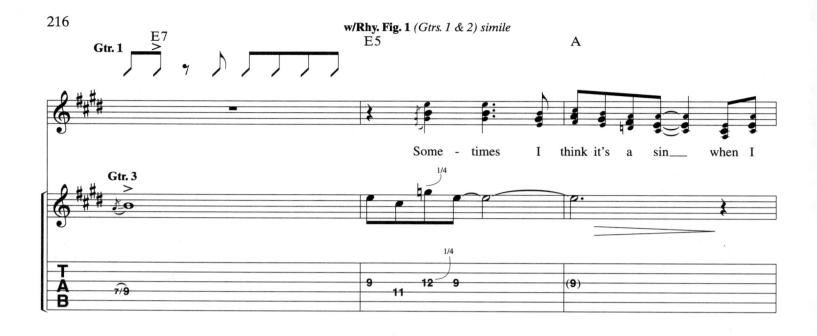
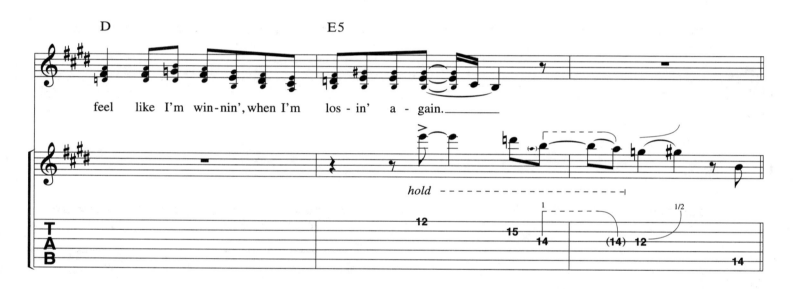

TIN MAN

217

Words and Music by
DEWEY BUNNELL

Moderately ♩ = 88

Intro:

Gtr. 1 (Acoustic)

Verse:

Cont. rhy. simile

Some-times___ late, when things are real and___ peo-ple share the gift of___ gab___ be-tween them-selves,___ some are___ quick to take the bait and___ catch the per-fect prize that___ waits___ a-mong the shelves. But

© 1970 (Renewed) WB MUSIC CORP.
All Rights Reserved

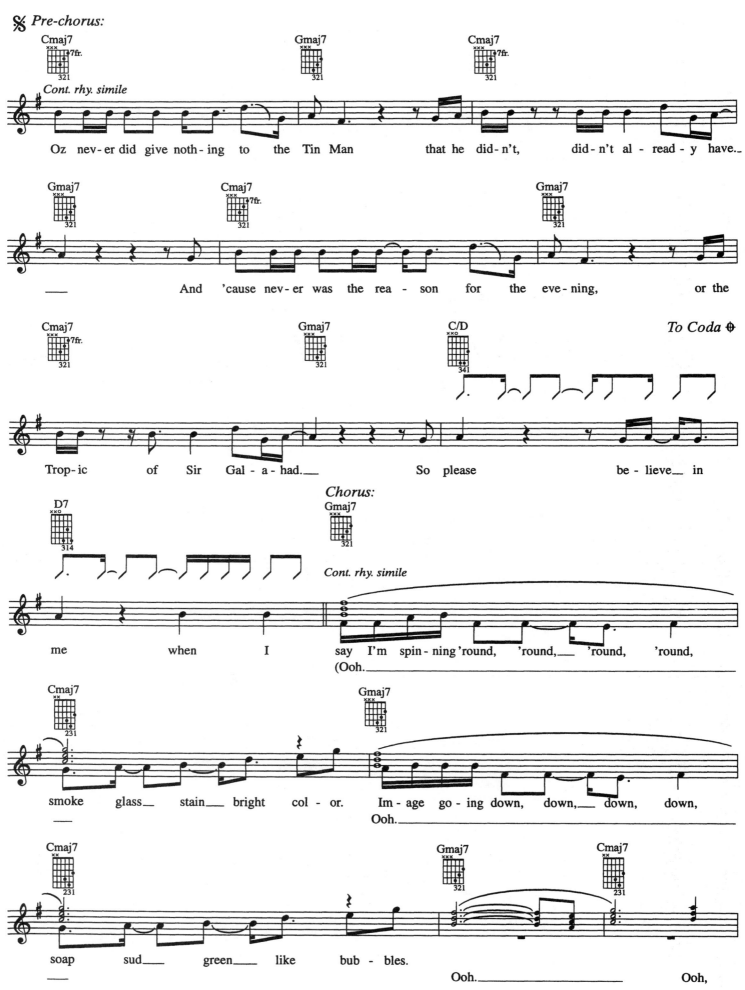

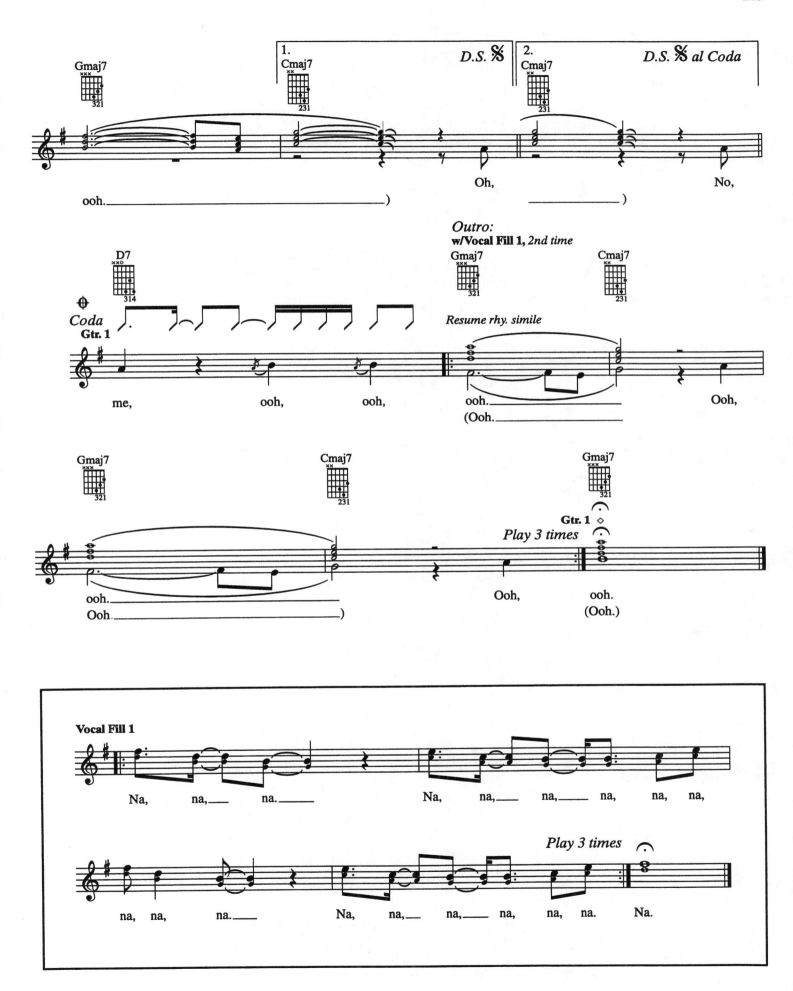

TAXI

Words and Music by HARRY CHAPIN

Moderately ♩ = 60

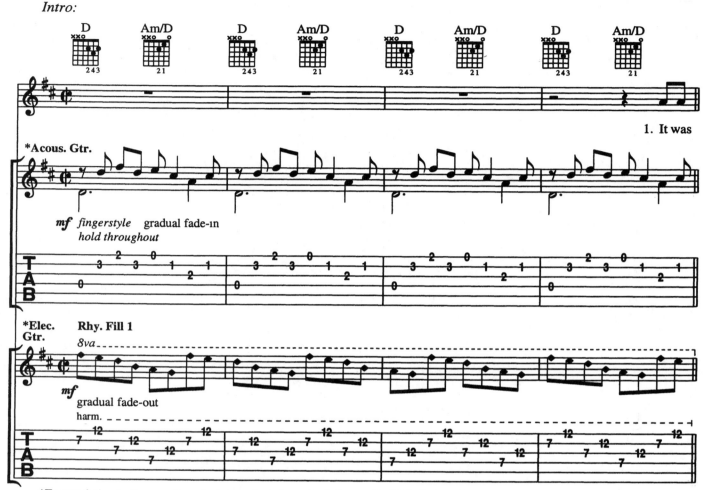

*To match the studio recording, de-tune guitars down 1 whole step D, G, C, F, A, and D, then place capo on 2nd fret after 2nd verse where indicated.

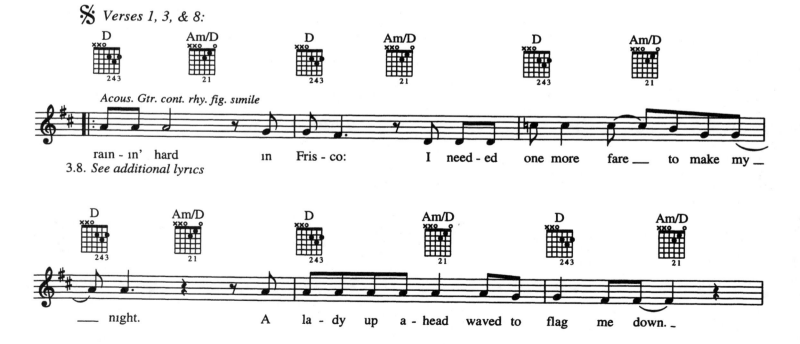

Verses 1, 3, & 8:

rain-in' hard in Fris-co: I need-ed one more fare to make my night. A la-dy up a-head waved to flag me down.

3.8. See additional lyrics

© 1972 (Renewed) STORY SONGS, LTD.
All Rights Administered by WB MUSIC CORP.
All Rights Reserved

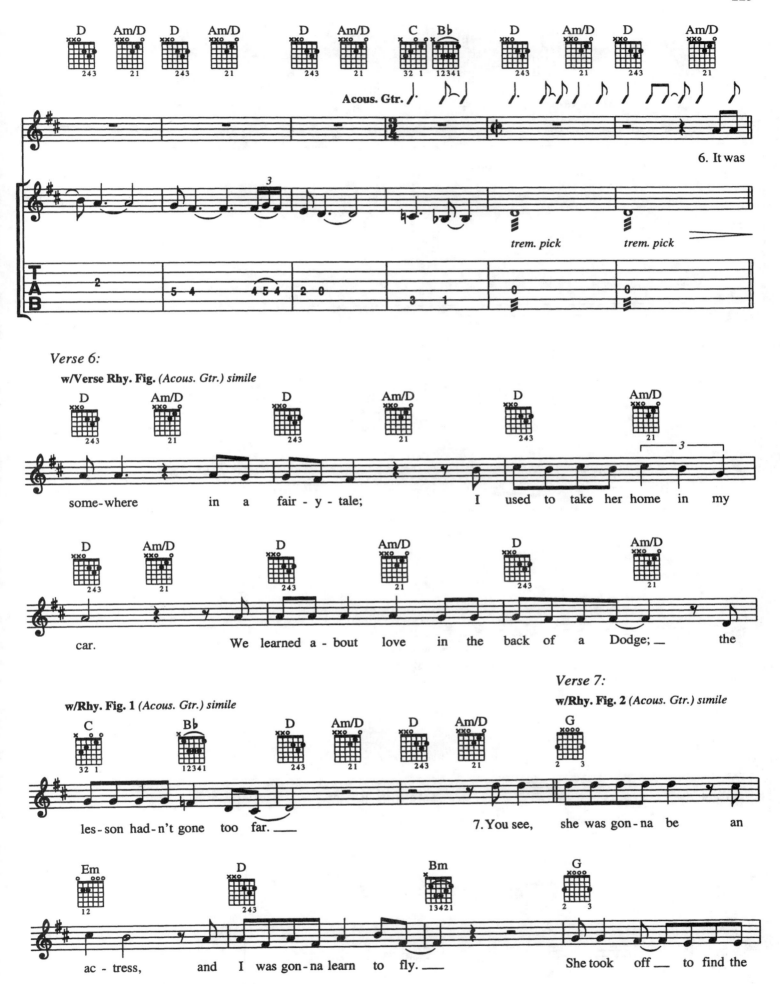

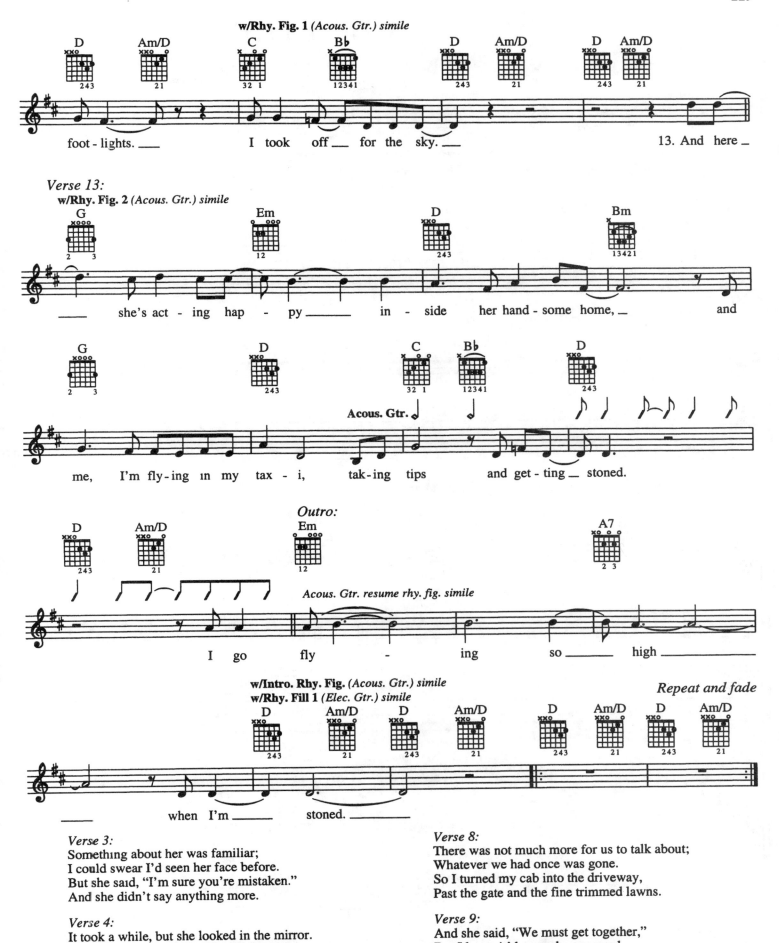

Verse 3:
Something about her was familiar;
I could swear I'd seen her face before.
But she said, "I'm sure you're mistaken."
And she didn't say anything more.

Verse 4:
It took a while, but she looked in the mirror.
Then she glanced at the license for my name.
A smile seemed to come to her slowly;
It was a sad smile just the same.

Verse 8:
There was not much more for us to talk about;
Whatever we had once was gone.
So I turned my cab into the driveway,
Past the gate and the fine trimmed lawns.

Verse 9:
And she said, "We must get together,"
But I knew it'd never be arranged.
Then she handed me twenty dollars for a two-fifty fare;
She said, *(spoken)* "Harry, keep the change."

TIME IN A BOTTLE

Words and Music by
JIM CROCE

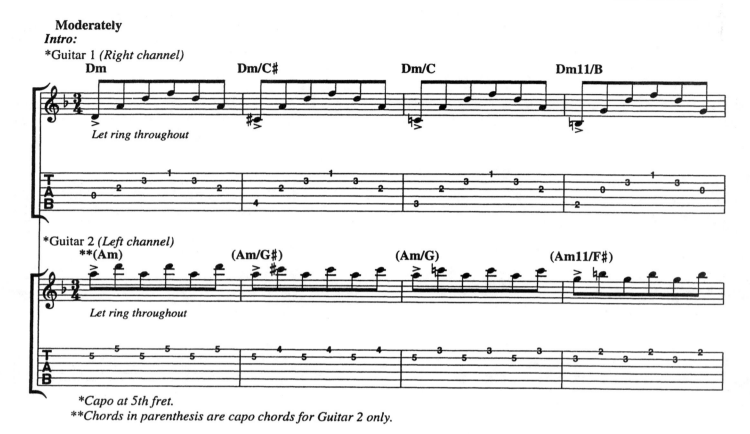

*Capo at 5th fret.
**Chords in parenthesis are capo chords for Guitar 2 only.

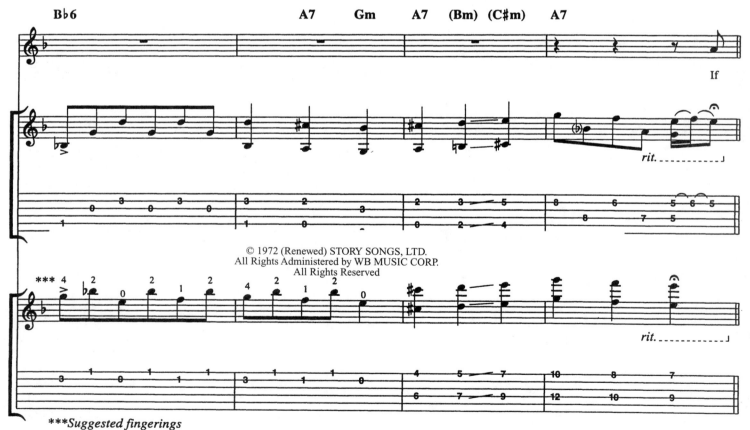

***Suggested fingerings

Time in a Bottle - 8 - 1

© 1972 DENJAC MUSIC COMPANY
© Renewed 2000 and Assigned to CROCE PUBLISHING in the U.S.A.
All Rights outside the U.S.A. Administered by DENJAC MUSIC COMPANY
All Rights Reserved

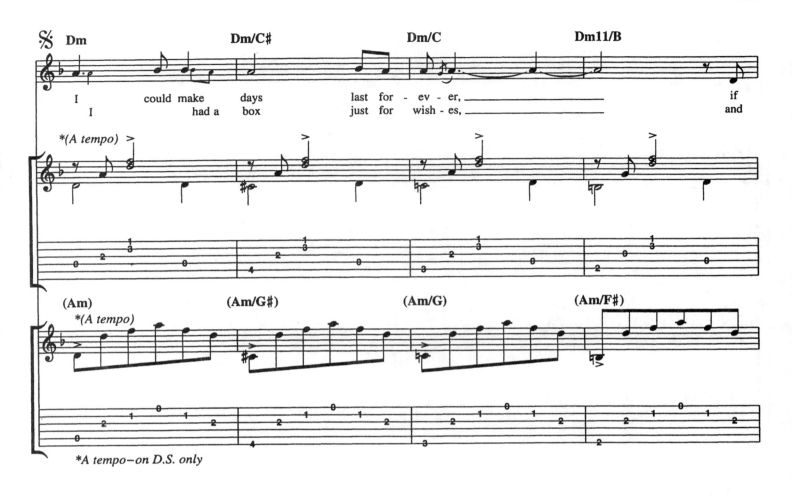
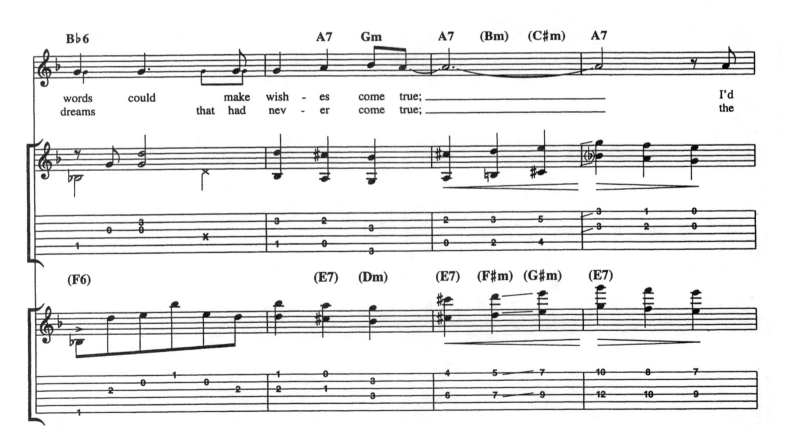

*A tempo—on D.S. only

Time in a Bottle - 8 - 4

Time in a Bottle - 8 - 5

235

Time in a Bottle - 8 - 6

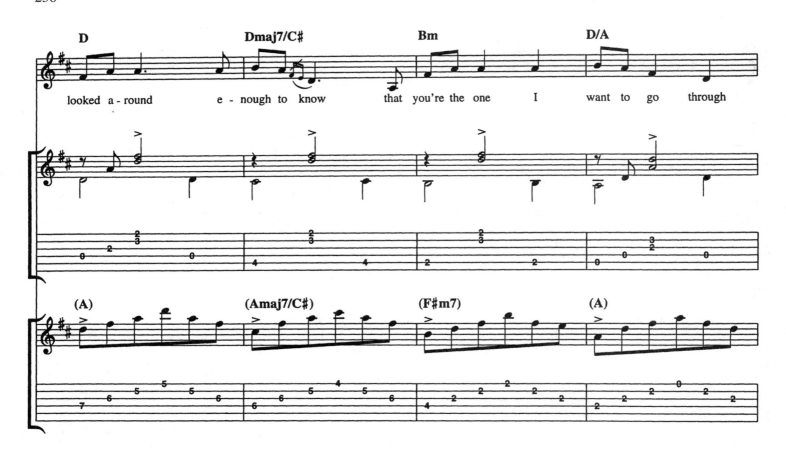
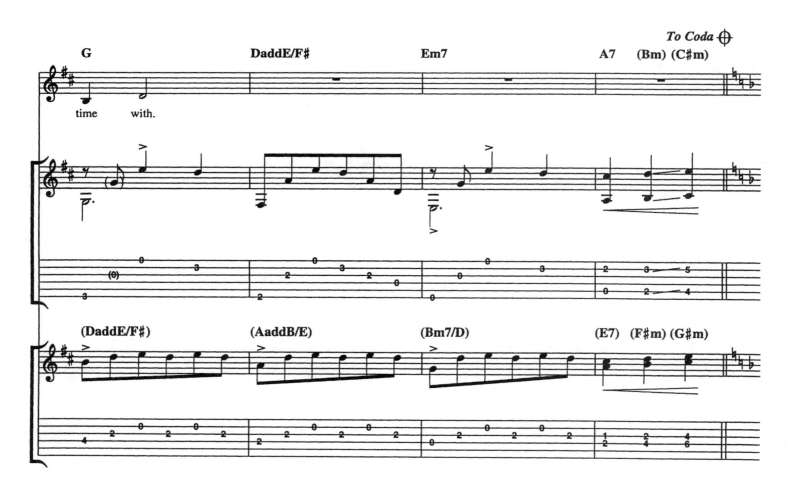

TUPELO HONEY

Words and Music by
VAN MORRISON

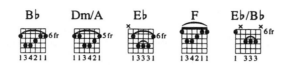

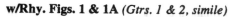

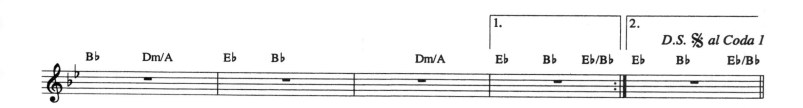

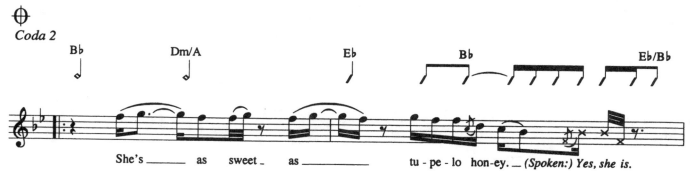

Tupelo Honey - 4 - 3

Verses 2 & 3:
You can't stop us
On the road to freedom.
You can't stop us
'Cause our eyes can see.
Men with insight,
Men of granite,
Knights in armor intent on chivalry.
(To Chorus:)

WILDFIRE

Words and Music by
MICHAEL MARTIN MURPHEY
and LARRY CANSLER

Tempo I (Slowly ♩ = 76)

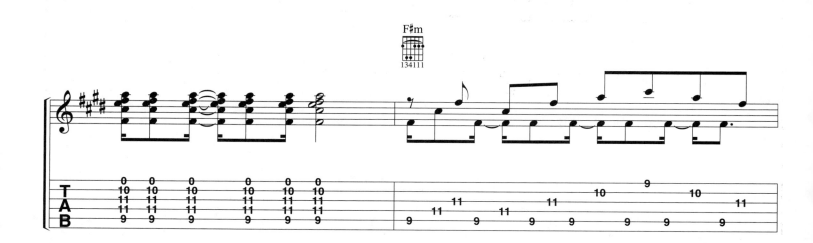
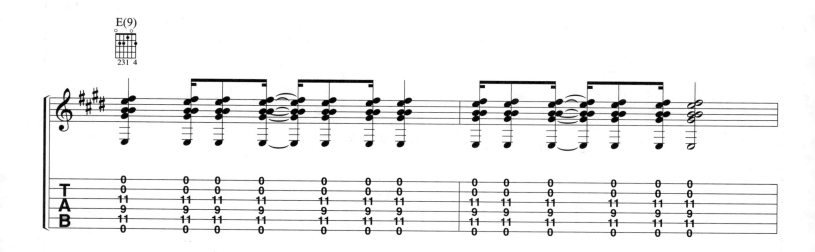

© 1975 WARNER-TAMERLANE PUBLISHING CORP.
All Rights Reserved

246

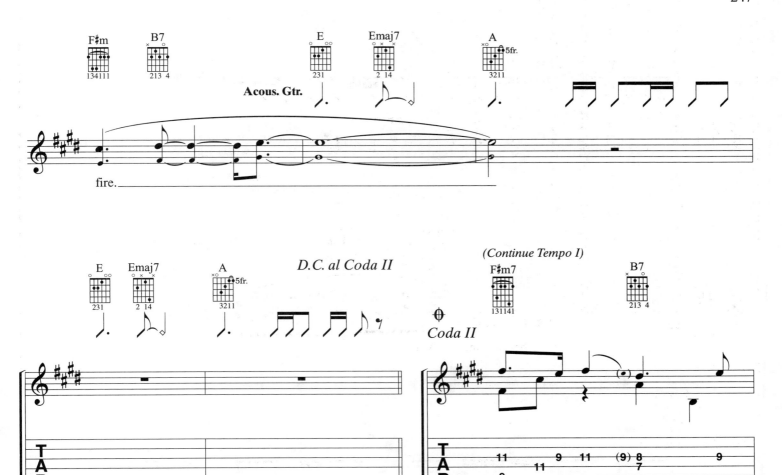

Wildfire - 6 - 6

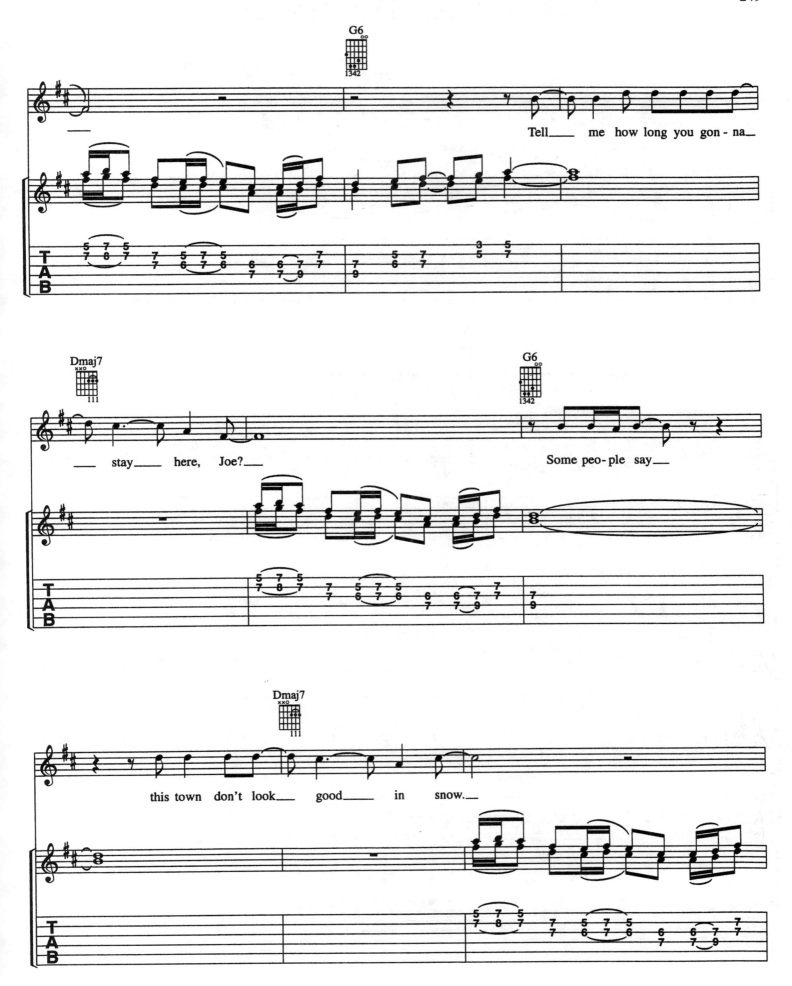

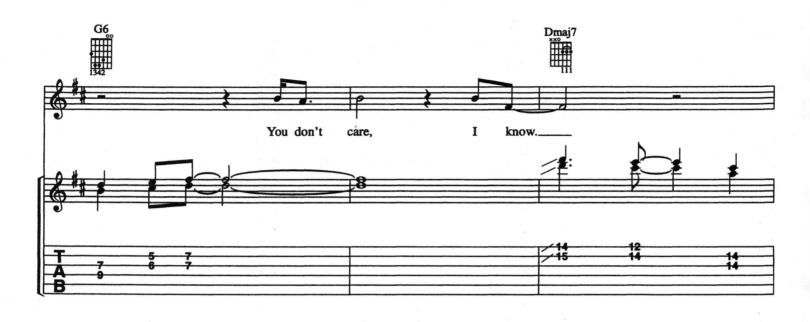
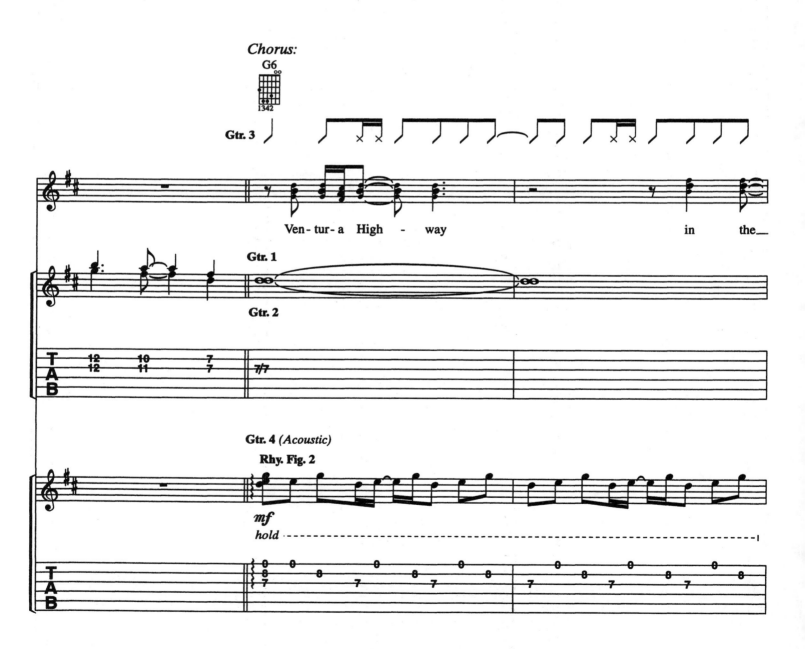

Verse 2:
Wishin' on a falling star,
Watchin' for the early train.
Sorry, boy, but I've been hit by
Purple rain.
Aw, come on, Joe, you can always
Change your name.
Thanks a lot, son, just the same.
(To Chorus:)

GUITAR TAB GLOSSARY

TABLATURE EXPLANATION
TAB illustrates the six strings of the guitar.
Notes and chords are indicated by the placement of fret numbers on each string.

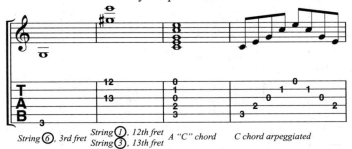

String ⑥, 3rd fret   String ①, 12th fret   A "C" chord   C chord arpeggiated
String ③, 13th fret

BENDING NOTES

Half Step: Play the note and bend string one half step (one fret).

Whole Step: Play the note and bend string one whole step (two frets).

Slight Bend/Quarter-Tone Bend: Play the note and bend string sharp.

Prebend (Ghost Bend): Bend to the specified note before the string is plucked.

Prebend and Release: Play the already-bent string, then immediately drop it down to the fretted note.

Unison Bends: Play both notes and immediately bend the lower note to the same pitch as the higher note.

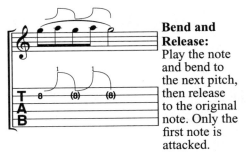

Bend and Release: Play the note and bend to the next pitch, then release to the original note. Only the first note is attacked.

Bends Involving More Than One String: Play the note and bend the string while playing an additional note on another string. Upon release, relieve the pressure from the additional note allowing the original note to sound alone.

Bends Involving Stationary Notes: Play both notes and immediately bend the lower note up to pitch. Return as indicated.

ARTICULATIONS

Hammer On: Play the lower note, then "hammer" your finger to the higher note. Only the first note is plucked.

Pull Off: Play the higher note with your first finger already in position on the lower note. Pull your finger off the first note with a strong downward motion that plucks the string—sounding the lower note.

Legato Slide: Play the first note and, keeping pressure applied on the string, slide up to the second note. The diagonal line shows that it is a slide and not a hammer-on or a pull-off.

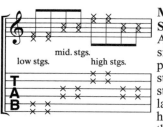

Muted Strings: A percussive sound is produced by striking the strings while laying the fret hand across them.

Palm Mute: The notes are muted (muffled) by placing the palm of the pick hand lightly on the strings, just in front of the bridge.

HARMONICS

Natural Harmonic: A finger of the fret hand lightly touches the string at the note indicated in the TAB and is plucked by the pick producing a bell-like sound called a harmonic.

RHYTHM SLASHES

Strum Marks/ Rhythm Slashes: Strum with the indicated rhythm pattern. Strum marks can be located above the staff or within the staff.

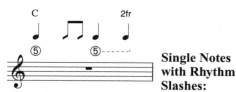

Single Notes with Rhythm Slashes: Sometimes single notes are incorporated into a strum pattern. The circled number is the string and the fret number is under that.

Artificial Harmonic: Fret the note at the first TAB number, lightly touch the string at the fret indicated in parens (usually 12 frets higher than the fretted note), then pluck the string with an available finger or your pick.

TREMOLO BAR

Specified Interval: The pitch of a note or chord is lowered to the specified interval and then return as indicated. The action of the tremolo bar is graphically represented by the peaks and valleys of the diagram.

Unspecified Interval: The pitch of a note or chord is lowered, usually very dramatically, until the pitch of the string becomes indeterminate.

PICK DIRECTION

Downstrokes and Upstrokes: The downstroke is indicated with this symbol (⊓) and the upstroke is indicated with this (V).